Christoph Breetz

Product packaging as a tool to demand a price premium

Does packaging enhance consumers' value perception to justify a price premium

Anchor Compact

Breetz, Christoph: Product packaging as a tool to demand a price premium: Does packaging enhance consumers' value perception to justify a price premium. Hamburg, Anchor Academic Publishing 2014

Original title of the thesis: The impact of product packaging on consumers' value perception: Does packaging enable retailers to take premium pricing with their retailer brand premium tier in the food segment in Germany?

Buch-ISBN: 978-3-95489-232-7
PDF-eBook-ISBN: 978-3-95489-732-2
Druck/Herstellung: Anchor Academic Publishing, Hamburg, 2014

Bibliografische Information der Deutschen Nationalbibliothek:
Die Deutsche Nationalbibliothek verzeichnet diese Publikation in der Deutschen Nationalbibliografie; detaillierte bibliografische Daten sind im Internet über http://dnb.d-nb.de abrufbar

Bibliographical Information of the German National Library:
The German National Library lists this publication in the German National Bibliography. Detailed bibliographic data can be found at: http://dnb.d-nb.de

© Anchor Academic Publishing, ein Imprint der Diplomica® Verlag GmbH
http://www.diplom.de, Hamburg 2014
Printed in Germany

Abstract

This study addresses the question of the impact of packaging to demand a price premium leveraging the example of retailer brand premium products in the food segment in Germany. Product tiering is a pricing structure that is commonly used by producers, in which consumers are segmented by willingness to pay for specific (added) product benefits. This is a way of maximizing utility for both consumers and producers, and is commonly already leveraged by producers of branded products, but lately also retailer brands, especially to enable growth outside the value tier. The role or packaging in the current literature is described as being a key influencer in the purchase decision making process, especially in-store.

This research uses a survey across grocery purchase decision makers in Germany to identify the relationship of packaging and willingness to pay across a sample of retailer brand Tier 1, Tier 2 and Tier 3 products as well as a branded product in four different grocery categories (ham, cheese, jam and ice cream). Additionally five demographic factors such as e.g. age are collected. The intent is to answer whether i) packaging currently justifies the premium price of retailer brand tier 1 products compared to other product tiers, ii) packaging justifies the tier 1 retailer brand price premium, and iii) demographics influence the willingness to pay a premium price.

Overall results indicate that the difference in packaging appeal can explain up to 35% of the willingness to pay for a retailer brand tier 1 product. However, results differ by grocery category and can't be easily generalized to the entire food segment, driven by the difference in perceived risk by the consumer. With regards to packaging as sole justification for the price the consumer is willing to pay for the retailer brand tier 1 product the research has not shown any meaningful correlation. Whilst some demographics such as the shopper profile, especially what is defined a loyal shopper in this research, household size, net income or age show a high association with a higher willingness to pay, this yet again can't be generalized across all categories. Only the loyal shopper profile was common across most categories for a general higher willingness to pay.

Table of contents

List of figures

1. Introduction

1.1. Arrangement of the study

The study is arranged into five chapters. Chapter 1 (Introduction) will provide an overview of the German trade and retailer brand environment and its development over the past five years. Based on this the research problem, hypothesis and questions are posed as well as the potential limitations of the research. Following, chapter 2 (Literature review) will discuss the existing literature on the role of packaging, the consumer purchase decision and the role and development of retailer brands. Chapter 3 (Research methodology) lays out the methods of analysis used in the paper and identifies methodological limitations and issues. The selected analysis approach requires quantitative data collection which is described. Further, any ethical limitations as well as the reliability, validity and potential for generalization of the findings are discussed. Chapter 4 (Quantitative analysis results and discussion) presents the analytical results of the collected data and presents the key findings and conclusions from the survey data. Lastly, chapter 5 (Conclusions and recommendations) provides a summary of the findings and conclusions of the previous chapters and places them in context, as well as recommendations for retailers as well as areas for future research.

1.2. The German trade and retailer brand environment

In the past years retailer brands have continued their share growth in the German trade environment and marked in 2012 a new record high value market share of 37,9% (+3,2 ppts. vs. 5yrs. ago and +0,8 ppts. vs. 2011). Whilst the low cost retailer brands, or also so called value retailer brands, stagnated at around 25% market share, the growth is coming from the mid and high tier retailer brands which have grown by +3,9 ppts. versus five years ago. This growth has been mainly delivered at the expense of non-market leading branded products in a category. Market leader brands are showing stable market shares.

Figure 1: Value market share development German trade based on *GFK (2012)*

The sales in the German food segment are dominated by four key retailers who account for 69% of the total food segment turnover based on the top 30 retailer sales. The number one and two Edeka group and Rewe group offer both: i) the traditional supermarket stores as well as ii) discounter stores (e.g. Netto by Edeka, Penny by Rewe). Both sell branded products as well as retailer brands, however the amount of products and brands is limited at discounter stores. Importantly, hard discounter Aldi represents with 12% a channel which so far was not open for branded products and hence limited to mainly low cost retailer brands, until recent in/out activities starting in 2013.

Figure 2: German retailer ranking according to food turnover *based on Lebensmittelzeitung (2013)*

Rank	Retailer	Turnover Food 2012 in million Euro	Turnover Food 2012 in % of Top 30	Food % of total turnover	Turnover 2012 in million Euro
1	Edeka-Gruppe, Hamburg	44.567	26%	90,5%	49.267
2	Rewe-Gruppe, Köln	26.225	16%	71,3%	36.766
3	Schwarz-Gruppe, Neckarsulm	24.084	14%	81,1%	29.700
4	Aldi Gruppe, Essen/Mülheim	20.931	12%	82,0%	25.525
5	Metro-Gruppe, Düsseldorf	11.311	7%	37,3%	30.362
6	Lekkerland, Frechen	8.182	5%	99,0%	8.265
7	dm, Karlsruhe	4.601	3%	90,0%	5.112
8	Rossmann, Burgwedel	4.005	2%	90,0%	4.450
9	Bartels-Langness, Kiel3)	2.802	2%	77,7%	3.607
10	Transgourmet, Neu-Isenburg	2.596	2%	86,4%	3.004

Consumers already associate especially the long-time existing value retailer brands such as ja! (Rewe), Gut & Günstig (Edeka) or also Tip (Real/Metro) with the respective retailer chains *(Berentzen, J.B. 2010)*. However, given their classification as mainly value brands they represent a segment which not necessarily stands for quality. In order to overcome this, retailers started to widen the portfolio of retailer brands introducing mid and high tier retailer brands. *Kumar, N., Steenkamp, J.B. (2007)* identified two types of mid and high tier retailer brands: premium lite retailer brands (rather mid-tier) and premium price retailer brands (high tier). Especially the latter pursues a quality leadership over branded products which should also justify a premium pricing, whilst premium lite retailer brands aim for the same quality but a cheaper price than national brands. Figure 3 below illustrates the lineup of retailer brand tiers at national retailer Rewe, who offers a fairly complete three tier retailer brand offering across key categories.

Figure 3: Overview of retailer brands and respective tiers at national retailer Rewe

Rewe retailer brands					
	Cheese	**Jam**	**Pudding**	**Ham**	**Tea**
Tier 1 - Feine Welt	Rewe Feine Welt Fleur de Biere	Rewe Feine Welt Sonnige Erdbeere	Rewe Feine Welt Crème au Chocolat	Rewe Feine Welt Kochschinken	Rewe Feine Welt Kräuter des Südens
Tier 2 - REWE	Rewe Weichkäse	Rewe Erdbeermarmelade	Rewe Schokopudding mit Sahne	Rewe Delikatess Metzgerschinken	Rewe Schwarztee Earl Grey
Tier 3 - ja!	Ja! Camembert	Ja! Erdbeermarmelade	Ja! Schokodessert mit Sahne	Ja! Delikatess Kochschinken	Ja! Ceylom Assam

An example from the UK where this differentiation is already well developed is Tesco, with Tesco Everyday Value (value tier), Tesco Brand (mid-tier) and Tesco Finest (premium tier). Especially the mid-tier (premium lite) category is also already well developed in Germany, with most national retailers, excluding hard discounters (like Aldi), carrying a low and mid-tier product which also has an effect on consumer quality perception.

For example, the *ARD (2013)* has conducted a consumer test with orange juice. The same orange juice was used for all samples, but the packages shown were from four different retailers (national retailers

Rewe and Edeka, discounters Aldi and Lidl) and partially in the case of Rewe and Edeka the mid-tier brand. Despite being the same orange juice the consumers voted Rewe and Edeka as the best tasting ones. In more formal terms, the packaging of a product acts as one of the elements in the consumer's quality and price cognition, which is referencing the willingness to pay more for a given product *(Brunso, K., et al. 2002)*. Also, consumers tend to rely on packaging when they make the in-store decision *(Silayoi, P., Speece, M. 2004)* which however is also related to the total brand perception. Ultimately, price influences the perception of quality of a product, but perception of quality (e.g. through packaging) also influences willingness to pay the price *(Imram, N. 1999)*. Given the increased importance of tier 1 retailer brands (premium) for retailers, the intention of this study is to further investigate the relationship between willingness to pay higher pricing and packaging in the grocery segment.

1.3. Research problem
In the past two decades retailer brands have been growing mainly behind the value retailer brands. However, growth rates have stalled since mid-2000 and retailers can only continue to grow their retailer brand market share by expanding their retailer brands also in higher class tiers. Given the higher price levels they effectively compete with branded products and need to deliver a high quality impression to justify the pricing. The literature suggests that packaging and pricing are strongly correlated and that as such retailers might be able to sustain a price premium for their tier 1 retailer brands behind a qualitative strong packaging. The quality perception might be influenced by underlying demographics such as age, gender or shopping behaviour.

1.4. Purpose of the research
The purpose of this research is to use an analysis-led approach to identify the effect of packaging on the price elasticity i.e. what the consumer is willing to pay for the product. This will be evaluated in the context of differently tiered retailer brands and respective branded products in various food categories.

1.5. Research questions
The main underlying research question is if retailers can succeed in demanding a price premium for their premium tier retailer brands behind premium packaging. The research question will be explored using a quantitative analysis approach. In order to approach the research question in more depth the following sub-research questions will be explored:

1. Are consumers willing to pay a price premium for retailer brand Tier 1 products compared to branded and retailer brands Tier 2 / Tier 3 products based on the packaging appeal?
2. Do current retailer brand tier 1 premium priced products justify their price premium based on the packaging impression?
3. Are there demographic specifications such as gender, age, household size, household income or shopping behaviour influencing the willingness to pay a premium price?

1.6. Limitations of the research
Provided the given limitations of this study, this study only covers four grocery categories with retailer brands of one specific retailer. Hence, the generalization to the total food industry might be limited. Further, there may be limitations such as cultural aspects that might affect the findings in one way or another. This research is specific to the German shopper and its cultural, social and political context.

Given that this could be a potential determinant of how acceptable the findings of this research are globally, this is a significant limitation on the possible generalization of results. The research approach is retrospective as it is based on products available in-market. However, there is no actual sales data available to compare the true in-market results of the products and hence the research relies on a consumer survey only.

2.   Literature review

2.1.   Arrangement of the chapter

This chapter provides an overview of the existing literature with key focus on the role of packaging, the consumer purchase decision and the role of retailer brands. The literature review is structured in three parts. The first part is investigating the role of packaging in the food segment and especially its relation to pricing, shelf impact and gaining a competitive advantage. Following the drivers of the purchase decision in the food segment are reviewed. Lastly, the chapter is then concluded with a review of the role of retailer of brands and recent trends leading to multi-tier retailer brand offerings.

2.2.   The Importance of packaging in the food segment

The core principle of this research is that packaging is an important factor of the food merchandising business. The first section of the literature review evaluates the role of packaging in the marketing mix and where it serves to create a competitive advantage. Following, the regulatory requirements for food packaging, including materials and information that must be included are reviewed. This acknowledges both the functional and the brand-building role of packaging in food merchandising.

2.2.1. Packaging in the marketing mix

The marketing mix is a loose framework of marketing strategies and attributes that is used as a working set of guidelines for a given product *(Drewniany, B.L., Jewler, A.J. 2011)*. It is often conceptualized as the '4Ps' (Product, Price, Placement and Promotion), which are aspects of the marketing offer that are perceived by the consumer *(Drewniany, B.L., Jewler, A.J. 2011)*. Packaging plays a particular role in the marketing mix, including brand building, offering price cues and providing shelf impact. This, if done in a consumer relevant way, should result in a competitive advantage from the packaging choice. This will be evaluated in the following detailed review.

2.2.1.1. *Building a brand with packaging*

One of the most important things to understand about packaging is the fact that it is one of the most visible representations of the product and brand. The brand can be defined as the set of associations that are generated by the product's physical attributes (like trademarks, symbols and packaging), including quality associations, social associations, sensory or emotional associations and previous brand experience *(Drewniany, B.L., Jewler, A.J. 2011)*. The brand is the fundamental aspect of how the product is presented to consumers and how consumers recognize their potential experience with the brand *(Drewniany, B.L., Jewler, A.J. 2011)*. Thus, it is particularly important to understand how the packaging of a product contributes to the development of the brand.

Branding is intended as a mean of product differentiation *(Grimes, A., Doole, I. 1998)*. Generally, product differentiation between closely related consumer products is considered to be relatively meaningless, since it does not refer to functional qualities or differences between products. However, *Grimes, A., Doole, I. (1998)* noted that previous research by *Carpenter et al. (1994)* had shown that consumers actually value the seemingly meaningless differentiation through packaging. A highly effective form of differentiation is the inclusion of pictures of the product on the package, which serves as a resource to communicate brand equity *(Underwood, R.L, Klein, N.M. 2002)*. According to *Underwood, R.L, Klein, N.M. (2002)* product pictures serve a number of purposes, they set consumer expectations for the brand, help them define the brand *as* a brand and improve assessment of the brand's suitability to meet consumer needs. Thus, in a way, pictures of the product itself (even though this may not serve to differentiate the product) can result in improved brand recognition for food products *(Underwood, R.L, Klein, N.M. 2002)*.

It is important to evaluate the impact of packaging for the specific target market, since the meaning assigned to packaging attributes can be variable. For example, one study that explored different perceptions of international brands in the UK and Taiwan found that the impact of color choices was very different between these two cultural contexts *(Grimes, A., Doole, I. 1998)*. These differences in color perceptions resulted in differences in brand equity perceptions for brands such as Pepsi and Marlboro *(Grimes, A., Doole, I. 1998)*. Thus, while packaging is important to branding, the meaning of packaging is neither consistent nor reliable across cultural boundaries. Furthermore, food products are commonly characterized by low product involvement and low brand loyalty *(Grunert, K.G., et al. 1996)*. This means that the power of the brand itself is relatively low and cannot be relied upon to generate significant increased sales *(Grunert, K.G., et al. 1996)*.

2.2.1.2. *Packaging as pricing criterion*

In the current literature packaging also serves as a criterion for consumers to determine whether the price is appropriate. Whilst the food quality remains a key criterion, the judgments are also driven by two other factors, i) information on the food packaging and ii) previous brand or product experience *(Steenkamp, J.E.M., Van Trijp, H.C.M. 1996)*. In more formal terms, the packaging of a product acts as one of the elements in the consumer's price cognition, which is related to the willingness to pay for a given product *(Brunso, K., et al. 2002)*. Some of the factors in consumer choice that may be communicated by the product packaging in order to influence price include hedonic and sensory elements (perceptions of taste of the product), quality, convenience and health *(Brunso, K., et al. 2002)*. This means that it is particularly important for the new customer to have a positive impression of the brand's quality through its packaging in order to justify its price.

There are various aspects of packaging that influence the price that consumers are willing to pay. For example, some consumers are willing to pay more for functional, natural, or healthy products. However, still some are unwilling to pay a price premium for these products *(Steenkamp, J.E.M., Van Trijp, H.C.M. 1996)*. The price of the product and the packaging may also set certain sensory expectations *(Deliza, R., MacFie, H. 1996)*. For example, products that have a higher price, accompanied by packages that imply a special sensory experience (such as a luxurious or rare product), may actually encourage purchase, while products that promised this experience without the accompanying higher price may not have such a strong impact *(Deliza, R., MacFie, H. 1996)*. Thus, the choice of packaging and price should be congruent in order to support an understanding of the premium product as being 'worth' the higher price. It is important to note that not all consumers want the cheapest possible products. Hence, fitting the price and packaging expectations congruently together can offer positive benefits even for a product that is not targeting cost leadership *(Drewniany, B.L., Jewler, A.J. 2011)*. Ultimately, price influences the perception of quality of a product, but perception of quality (e.g. through packaging) also influence willingness to pay *(Imram, N. 1999)*.

There are a number of different ways to communicate the price directly via packaging. One such possibility is a price flash, where the price is displayed prominently on the packaging *(Rettie, R., Brewer, C. 2000)*. This is often done when a product is offered at a special price and when placed on the left has a moderate positive impact on recall of the product and price *(Rettie, R., Brewer, C. 2000)*. This type of direct display may not be the most effective, but it does have the advantage of increasing the consumer awareness of the product's price. Other approaches, including shelf labeling, are also factors in regulatory management, discussed below.

2.2.1.3. *Importance of packaging in-store (shelf impact)*

The importance of the packaging of a given product in-store is that it serves to distinguish very similar products from each other *(Rundh, B. 2009)*. So-called shelf impact refers to the ability of the product to stand out from competing products displayed nearby and is primarily driven by the colors, shapes and other characteristics of the product packaging *(Klimchuk, M.R., Krasovec, S.A. 2013)*. However, simply being different is insufficient to effectively provide shelf impact; instead the products need to be different in a way that makes them appealing to the consumer *(Klimchuk, M.R., Krasovec, S.A. 2013)*. Ultimately, as *Klimchuk, M.R., Krasovec, S.A. (2013)* note, the consumer will come to select a preferred product based on its color and packaging shape. Hence, controlling this aspect of the packaging and making it as appealing as possible is an important part of the product mix.

A number of studies have shown that choice of products is largely dependent on easily identifiable and positive aspects of the product, such as product packaging. A study in preschoolers suggests that packaging choice is to some extent individualistic and driven by favorite colors and personal preferences *(Marshall, D. et al. 2006)*. However, other studies have shown that the importance of color is much more consistent for adult consumers. In particular, adult consumers have undergone associative learning processes that have cemented consistent color meanings and implications *(Grossman, R.P., Wisenblit, J.W. 1999)*. This means that as adults, consumers are no longer driven by idiosyncratic personal preferences, but instead have more consistent responses informed by culture and previous experience *(Grossman, R.P., Wisenblit, J.W. 1999)*. Of course, this does mean that color associations are culturally variable, as shown by the study of UK and Taiwan consumers and their color associations *(Grimes, A., Doole, I. 1998)*. However, it is generally the case that by using color perceptions and associations within a culture, packaging can represent various aspects of the product in an immediate fashion.

The graphics and colors used on packaging may be even more important for shelf impact than the verbiage *(Bone, P.F., France, K. 2001)*. *Bone, P.F., France, K. (2001)* suggested that vividness and confirmation bias associated with colors and images on packaging have a much stronger impact on consumer choice in the store than wording on the package, which may not be absorbed under conditions of rapid selection. Their study found that even when specific verbal information was offered on the package (such as mitigation of health claims), images and colors resulted in a different understanding of the value of the product than the verbiage offered *(Bone, P.F., France, K. 2001)*. This study suggests that, although verbiage is important, in terms of immediate impact on the consumer in the store, packaging colors and graphics are far more relevant *(Bone, P.F., France, K. 2001)*.

2.2.1.4. *Gaining competitive advantage from packaging*

The ultimate question for marketers is, whether packaging actually represents a competitive advantage. Competitive advantage can be defined briefly as a characteristic or resource of the product that is valuable, rare, inimitable and non-substitutable *(Drewniany, B.L., Jewler, A.J. 2011)*. Most importantly, the competitive advantage increases the sales of the products. In consumer-led food product development, in which market-oriented firms identify needs from consumers themselves and seek to meet them *(Costa, A.I.A., Jongen, W.M.F. 2006)*, packaging may be particularly important because it illustrates the precise needs that are being met by the product *(Grunert, K.G. et al. 1996)*.

Packaging is an important element of competitive advantage because it is fundamental to consumer acceptance of the food product, influencing perceptions of safety, quality and sensory aspects of the food contained within it *(Imram, N. 1999)*. The package offers competitive advantage because it is a primary mechanism for communication to consumers about these aspects of the product, as well as how it may be best used, how it is differentiated from competitors and what benefits the consumer may gain from its use *(Nancarrow, G. et al. 1998)*. These communications are not just surrounding sensory experience. For example, communications about health on food packaging may play into social discourses on healthy eating and dietary needs, making the product either more or less desirable to a certain group of people *(Bech-Larsen, T., Scholderer, J. 2007; Chrsyochou, P., et al. 2010)*. Packaging can allow for functional foods (or those that are marketed as serving a further purpose than general nutrition or sensory aspects of the eating experience) to communicate and differentiate themselves from others based on these refined characteristics, although care must be taken not to make unsupportable or illegal claims *(Bech-Larsen, T., Scholderer, J. 2007)*. This offers a potentially large benefit for the marketer of such foods in developing consumer desire for its products.

In addition to its selling role, packaging also plays a logistical role in maintaining competitive advantage *(Rundh, B. 2005)*. For example, packaging can extend the shelf life of products or make them more easily traceable, making them more appealing to retailers as well as consumers *(Dainelli, D. et al. 2008; Rundh, B. 2005)*. Packaging also encourages interaction between the consumer and the product; by looking at and reading packages, the consumer becomes aware of the product and its potential benefits *(Rundh, B. 2009)*. This offers a potential significant competitive advantage for the firm that can encourage this interaction. There are some tricks that can be used in this case. For example, by placing non-verbal information (images) on the left and verbal information on the right, package designers can create situations where consumers can accommodate both types of information more rapidly *(Rettie, R., Brewer, C. 2000)*. These types of design aspects of the package can generate competitive advantage by making them stand out more from competitors and improving consumer understanding.

2.2.2. Regulatory aspects of food packaging

In addition to its marketing information, food packaging plays a number of other roles. For example, it protects and preserves food, provides tamper protection and indicates food waste reduction *(Marsh, K., Bugusu, B. 2007)*. Many of these roles are enhanced by the choice of material (such as metal, plastics, or paperboard); however, the choice of material can also lead to excessive packaging, which creates a waste problem and can cause disposal difficulties *(Marsh, K., Bugusu, B. 2007)*. This makes functional characteristics and solid waste disposal a key area of packaging regulation, although the precise regulations vary by jurisdiction. For example, many states and countries have bottle deposit rules, which encourage post-consumer recycling *(Marsh, K., Bugusu, B. 2007)*. Others limit the types of materials that can be used in packaging, in order to control the amount of hard to recycle packaging that ends up in landfills *(Marsh, K., Bugusu, B. 2007)*.

Difference in regulatory regimes mean that packages sometimes must be redesigned multiple times for international markets *(Heckman, J.H. 2005)*. Heckman, J.H. (2005) compares food packaging content regulation in the United States and European Union, citing a number of differences in these regulatory regimes. He notes that there are similar requirements for testing of materials, although toxicity thresholds and specific tests used may differ *(Heckman, J.H. 2005)*. Thus, there may be differences in whether a given packaging material is allowed in the US and EU *(Heckman, J.H. 2005)*

New types of packaging also pose a regulatory challenge. Active and intelligent food packaging, which is a novel type of packaging that reacts environmentally to extend the life of food and directly indicate freshness using a monitoring system, also poses a regulatory challenge *(Dainelli, D. et al. 2008)*. This type of packaging may use nanotechnology to prolong shelf life of products, while intelligent labels may indicate freshness *(Dainelli, D. et al. 2008)*. These would clearly be positive factors for marketing, but the regulatory implications of this type of packaging have not yet been fully resolved.

A further regulatory issue in food packaging is required information. For example, nutritional information has been required on most food packages sold in the United States since 1990 *(Underwood, R.L., Ozanne, J.L. 1998)*. Nutritional labeling is also required in the EU *(Cheftel, J.C. 2005)*. There are also other regulatory package labeling requirements, including size and volume requirements *(Underwood, R.L., Ozanne, J.L. 1998)*. Other verbal claims on packaging that may be regulated include nutritional and origin claims (such as 'organic' and 'low-fat'), allergens or potential allergens, suitability for special diets and ingredient information *(Cheftel, J.C. 2005)*. Overall, the regulatory environment (which may vary depending on the market) means that use of packaging materials and information may be constrained.

2.3. Consumers and the purchase decision in the food segment

While product packaging is particularly important in the marketing mix, the most important point is the role of packaging in the formation of consumer expectations and its ultimate role in the decision to purchase a given product. Thus, understanding consumer expectations and packaging's role in their formation, as well as understanding the actual purchase decision, is fundamental in understanding how packaging influences the actual purchase decision.

2.3.1. Influence of packaging on consumer expectations

There have been a number of studies done on how packaging influences consumer expectations of a given product. These studies generally show that the choice of wording, images and colors on product packaging set sensory and other expectations for the product.

The images included on food packaging serve as one factor in setting consumer expectations. A study on orange juice cartons revealed that the choice of image actually influenced the consumer's sensory assessment of the product *(Mizutani, N., et al. 2010)*. Mizutani, N., et al. (2010) used four different sets of images to represent orange juice with different pleasantness and congruence characteristics. They then performed a taste test (using the same orange juice) to determine the effects on taste. The authors found that pleasant packaging images resulted in perceptions that the juice was fresher and more palatable, while those with pleasant congruent images were also rated as having a better aroma *(Mizutani, N., et al. 2010)*. This study strongly suggests that package imagery can generate consumer perceptions and expectations of the sensory experience of the product.

There is also evidence that the shape and color of packaging will play a role in setting consumer expectations. One study found that packaging resulted in sensory perception differences, although these differences were modulated by the individual's sensitivity to design *(Becker, L., et al. 2011)*. Becker, L., et al. (2011) studied the perception of 'tough' yogurt containers (as indicated by different curvatures and coloration of the container) and its effect on consumer expectations of taste. They found that the designs that were bolder did result in a difference in taste expectations and experience by consumers *(Becker, L., et al. 2011)*. A second study on milk desserts also found that the shape and color of the packaging was a relevant aspect of the consumer expectation *(Ares, G., Deliza, L. 2010)*. Ares, G., Deliza, L. (2010) designed six packages with varying shapes and coloration for the same milk dessert and then asked consumers to rate them based on expectations of liking and sensory expectations. They found that consumers associated different packaging colors with different flavors; for example, cream was associated with dulce de leche (sweet, delicious), while black was associated with bitter chocolate (disgusting, interesting) *(Ares, G., Deliza, L. 2010)*. Shape was also important, with square packages being viewed more positively and round packages being viewed as runny or disgusting *(Ares, G., Deliza, L. 2010)*. This study provides direct evidence that the choice of packaging will influence the consumer's expectation of the product. A third study of Cheddar cheese packaging also showed that package attributes, including color, shape and wording, influenced the sensory perception of the contents *(Murray, J.M., Delahunty, C.M. 2000)*.

Volume perceptions related to the shape of the packaging are also a potential factor in setting consumer expectations *(Raghubir, P., Krishna, A. 1999)*. Raghubir, P., Krishna, A. (1999) tested seven different packaging configurations with different shape and height characteristics, in order to determine the effect on consumer perceptions and expectations. They found that the height of the product packaging was the simplest heuristic used by consumers to guess at the total volume of the package *(Raghubir, P., Krishna, A. 1999)*. Furthermore, they also found that perceived value was influenced by height, with reduced height being associated with reduced perceived consumption *(Raghubir, P., Krishna, A. 1999)*. Overall, they indicated that the height and perceived volume of the packaging influenced perceived consumption and satisfaction with the product, even though in all cases consumers had access to containers of the same absolute volume *(Raghubir, P., Krishna, A. 1999)*. Thus, shape of the container is not just an aesthetic perception, but also related to the functional value and potential satisfaction experienced by the consumer.

Sometimes, packaging choices may set up contradictory consumer expectations. For example, a study of health claims on packaging in Nordic countries found that the presence of a health claim tended to reduce consumer expectations of other characteristics, like naturalness and taste *(Lahteenmaki, L. et al. 2010)*. This study also suggested that health claims do not necessarily increase perceptions of the healthiness of the product, even though it may negatively impact other perceptions *(Lahteenmaki, L. et al. 2010)*. Thus, marketers need to choose their packaging claims carefully in order to prevent conflict between claims reducing the power of the primary claim.

2.3.2. What drives the purchase decision in-store

While packaging clearly influences consumer expectations of the product, this does not fully explain how consumers make decisions in-store. There have been a number of approaches to answer this question.

One study of milk desserts focused on product involvement and attitude to packaging characteristics as a driver of the in-store purchase decision *(Ares, G. et al. 2010)*. Ares, G., et al. (2010) found that product involvement (or the extent to which a consumer will think about a purchase) was a factor in determining how a consumer will assess willingness to purchase. The authors used a series of different packages for chocolate milk desserts, varying between hedonic and functional attributes and with different package shapes, colors, brands and pictures *(Ares, G. et al. 2010)*. They compared perception pairs such as useless/useful and mundane/fascinating to determine how interested the individuals were in the product; additionally they assessed the importance of the functional claim of high levels of anti-oxidants *(Ares, G. et al. 2010)*. The authors found that willingness to purchase the product was driven both by high involvement (or the extent to which the purchase was interesting or important) and the personal importance of the anti-oxidant claim *(Ares, G. et al. 2010)*. Thus, the packaging and its claims is a clear factor in the in-store purchase decision.

It is not only involvement that contributes to in-store purchasing decisions. A study of packaging influences on in-store decision making found that time pressure also played a role in the decision process *(Silayoi, P., Speece, M. 2004)*. *Silayoi, P., Speece, M. (2004)* concluded that consumers relied on packaging cues in order to make in-store decisions, especially when they were hurried and did not have much involvement with the purchase decision. The consumers in their focus groups suggested that package wording was important, but also that complicated package wording could actually impede decision making in-store, especially in environments when they were rushed *(Silayoi, P., Speece, M. 2004)*. This suggests that, once again involvement is key, but also that consumer resources like time and attention play a role in determining the outcomes of the purchase decision.

Finally, environmental cues and the in-store experience can influence the purchase decision *(Bellizzi, J.A., Hite, R.E. 1992)*. *Bellizzi, J.A., Hite, R.E. (1992)* tested two simulated retail environments, one primarily blue (denoting calmness and coolness) and one primarily red (denoting tenseness and negativity). They found that the blue environment resulted in more immediate purchases and fewer postponements than the red environment *(Bellizzi, J.A., Hite, R.E. 1992)*. This is a very basic finding about the importance of the store environment on the purchase, but it points to a very important aspect that needs to be understood. Not all purchasing factors are under the control of the marketer. Uncontrolled environmental factors need to be taken into account when considering the consumer purchase decision.

2.4. Retailer Brands and the shopper in the food segment

The final focus of this literature review is an exploration of why consumers buy retailer brands. Retailer or private label brand products are produced by the retailer for in-store sales, hence they may have a distinct brand identity from the store *(Grunert, K.G. et al. 1996)*. The actual supply chain for retailer branded products is often similar to (or even identical to) national branded products, though retailer policies on quality and consistency of goods may vary *(Grunert, K.G. et al. 1996)*.

Most of the examples of packaging design that are held out as positively influencing consumer decision making are from large-scale international brands, which are marketed to a wide range of individuals and markets. However, retailer brands are not widely marketed and may not have as much marketing support or multi-faceted development behind them. In this section, the consumer motivations for purchase of retailer brands and a recent movement away from the value brand paradigm of the retailer brand are discussed as a mean of understanding better the increasing complexity within this sector.

2.4.1. Why do consumers buy retailer brands?

There have been a number of studies why consumers buy retailer or private label brands. While many of these studies focus on price (and related issues), other aspects of the brand choice include perceptions of quality and brand loyalty. It should be noted that packaging, while it is seen as an area for improvement by retailers, is not necessarily viewed as a strength or determining feature in the selection of products, unlike for national brands *(Garrettson, J.A. et al. 2002)*. However, this does not necessarily indicate that packaging is unimportant.

One study focused on the choice of retailer brands as a risk assessment exercise *(Batra, R., Sinha, I. 2000)*. The authors posited that the selection of retailer brands was associated with a certain amount of risk and found that the willingness to purchase was increased when there was a reduction in perceived risk *(Batra, R., Sinha, I. 2000)*. The authors found that purchase of retailer brands was more commonly associated with products that had high 'search' characteristics (or need for information that could be imparted on the product package) *(Batra, R., Sinha, I. 2000)*. This reduced the uncertainty about consumption, particularly for the initial purchase and made consumers more willing to purchase *(Batra, R., Sinha, I. 2000)*.

In addition to information and risk, several studies have addressed the role of price in the selection of retailer and private label brands. *Batra, R., Sinha, I. (2000)* found that price was actually a concern for the selection of both private label and national brands. In earlier research, the authors had found that price was a significant determinant of the choice of private label brands *(Sinha, I., Batra, R. 1999)*. This was particularly true in two categories of goods (which may or may not overlap). The first category of goods was goods with a relatively low risk profile, or where the consumer was not in serious doubt about the potential quality of the private label product *(Sinha, I., Batra, R. 1999)*. The second category of goods was where there was a high degree of perceived unfairness in the price of the national brand, which increased consumer resistance to the national brand and willingness to seek alternatives *(Sinha, I., Batra, R. 1999)*. Obviously, not every potential retailer branded product might fall into these categories, but a large number of such products will be relevant. A second study indicates that external factors like business cycles (recessions) may increase the attractiveness of private label goods, because falling incomes mean that the price differentials between private label and national brands become much more relevant to consumers *(Lamey, I., et al. 2007)*. Furthermore, these switches are 'sticky,' in that consumers change readily to store brands during recession, but may not change as rapidly back to national brands following economic recovery *(Lamey, I., et al. 2007)*. Thus, the set of price-related circumstances that influence consumers to buy retailer brands includes *both* perceptions of price unfairness and relative consumer income.

A third category of influences on the choice of retailer brands is retailer-related characteristics, including perceived quality, store aesthetics and store loyalty. *DelVecchio, D. (2001)* study indicated that consumers that imbued brands with more symbolic meaning were more likely to consider private brands more effectively, but only when these private brands were competing in categories of goods that were largely private in nature. In categories of goods that had a high level of existing branding and national brand competition, the private brand may not be considered to be as strongly quality-driven and may not have the brand recognition power associated with national brands *(DelVecchio, D. 2001)*. Thus, perceived quality and its power depends on the characteristics of the market as well as the product. The aesthetic nature of the store itself also influences the perception of quality of the associated store brand *(Richardson, P., et al. 1996)*. In particular, retail environments that were more positive aesthetically (cleaner, less crowded and more harmonious colors) were associated with stronger acceptance of their retailer brands *(Richardson, P., et al. 1996)*. A third aspect of private label use is existing store loyalty, or the extent to which consumers choose to shop at a given store *(Ailawadi, K.L., et al. 2008)*. *Ailawadi, K.L., et al. (2008)* found that higher levels of private label use were associated with increased store loyalty and vice versa, suggesting a strong relationship between these two areas. Looking back to *Batra, R., Sinha, I. (2000)* framework for use of private labels, it is possible that the increased in-store loyalty reduces perceived risk for private label goods and increases the experience information available about the private label, which significantly reduces the barrier to purchase a private label.

2.4.2. Recent trends in Retailer Brands – Moving from value brands to multi-tier offerings

Although private label brands have traditionally inhabited the value section of the supermarket, there have been a number of trends that have been moving retailers away from this segment only and into multi-tier offerings. One factor in this revision of the position of retailer brands is the recognition that they offer potential competitive advantage and category profitability, particularly in categories that are not heavily targeted by national brands *(Pepe, M.S., et al. 2012)*. This offers an incentive to retailers to develop multiple positions in the market and meet multiple market needs *(Pepe, M.S., et al. 2012)*. Pepe, *M.S., et al. (2012)* found that category profitability was not strongly affected by private-label focus in the outcomes of one supermarket, but still observed that developing a strong private label brand strategy was one of the ways in which supermarkets could increase overall profitability. One of the major trends in expanding retail brands has been the development of multi-tier offerings, which allow consumers to select preferred levels of quality and price as well as variety *(Lincoln, K., Thomassen, L. 2009)*. *Berentzen, J.B. (2010)* identified four generations of retailer brands, which have evolved over the past decades.

Figure 4: Generations of retailer brands based on *Berentzen, J.B. (2010)*

	Generation			
	First	**Second**	**Third**	**Fourth**
Classification	Hard discounter retailer brands	Low cost retailer brands	Brand identity linked to retailer	Premium price store brands
Pricing	Value pricing	Value pricing	Value / Mid-tier pricing	Premium pricing
Quality / Innovation	As cheap as possible, low quality	In line with Tier 3 brands, often imitate packaging	Quality improvement, not sole cost leadership	Quality leadership

For example, UK supermarket chain Tesco's private label goods are collectively the largest consumer brand in the world; however, this growth is not driven by a single monolithic brand, but instead by a number of variations of quality and price *(Lincoln, K., Thomassen, L. 2009)*. These products range from the Tesco value range (which offers a limited selection basic packaging and basic quality goods) to Tesco Finest (which has more sophisticated packaging, higher-quality ingredients and luxury products and recipes) *(Lincoln, K., Thomassen, L. 2009)*. In some cases, retailer brands are generally higher-level; for example, US supermarket Trader Joe's offers primarily own-brand gourmet products, none of which are positioned as basic or value goods *(Abraham, S. 2005)*. This trend is not being followed by all retailers that offer private label brands, especially those in the cost leader position. For example, German hard discounter Aldi still pursues a cost leader private brand strategy, offering a basic selection of goods at a single quality *(Lincoln, K., Thomassen, L. 2009)*. Overall, however, large retailers (e.g. Rewe or Edeka in Germany) are moving toward the use of multi-tier brands that represent different levels of performance, perceived quality and price in order to capture more of the consumer market. This is considered to be one of the main areas for development of retail brands *(Lincoln, K., Thomassen, L. 2009)*.

2.5. Conclusions from the literature review

Importantly, the review of the current literature confirms the validity of the research question as they build upon the existing understanding in the literature, but as such have not been penetrated in great detail.

The current literature confirms a strong link of packaging within overall brand equity, but also that it is one part of consumer's price cognition.

There is a clear indication that brand building and brand perception is to some extend linked to the packaging as pointed out by *Drewniany, B.L., Jewler, A.J. (2011)*. With regards to a possible impact of packaging on willingness to pay / pricing *Brunso, K., et al. (2002)* confirm this in their work and indicate packaging as one of the elements in the consumer's price cognition. *Deliza, R., MacFie, H. (1996)* show that packaging and price are in close relationship as a product with a luxurious packaging and a high price is more successful than even a luxurious product with a low price. Ultimately, price influences the perception of the quality of a product, but perception of quality (e.g. through packaging) also influence willingness to pay *(Imram, N. 1999)*. In summary, the literature confirms that there is a strong relationship between pricing and packaging.

Packaging acts as key enabler for product differentiation and creates consumer expectations

Besides the general relationship of packaging and price the literature identifies packaging as a key enabler for differentiation. The shelf impact of a packaging in-store heavily relies on the colors, shapes and other characteristics of the product packaging *(Klimchuk, M.R., Krasovec, S.A. 2013 and Bone, P.F., France, K. 2001)* and serves as a consumer relevant mean of differentitation according to *Carpenter et al. (1994)*. Further, the study conducted by *Mizutani, N., et al. (2010)* concludes that package imagery can generate consumer perceptions and expectations of the sensory experience of the product. Hence, in summary it is valid to conclude that the current literature supports the theory of packaging to support the respective pricing strategy (tier level).

Retailer brands still have to overcome a consumer perceived barrier of risk which might be overcome by pricing, retailer image or being a low risk product.

The key barrier retailer brands have to overcome is the amount of perceived risk by the consumer when buying a retailer brand *(Batra, R., Sinha, I. 2000)*. In total there are three main categories why people buy retailer brands:

1) Low risk products don't provide the burden of risk *(Batra, R., Sinha, I. 2000)*
2) Too high price premium between national brand and retailer brand *(Batra, R., Sinha, I. 2000)*
3) Strong quality perception of the retailer selling the retailer brand *(Richardson, P., et al. 1996)*

Once consumers switched to a retailer brand, even if e.g. for monetary/value reasons solely during recession, they may not change as rapidly back to national brands *(Lamey, I., et al. 2007)* if not dissatisfied with the product as such.

3. Research methodology

3.1. Arrangement of the chapter

The following chapter will present the research approach, by first introducing the overall research methodology which is then followed by the specific level of research. Afterwards an overview of the population and sample size is provided, which is followed by a description of the data collection, analysis and presentation. Lastly, potential ethical concerns are raised and perspective on data reliability, validity and generalization is provided.

3.2. Research approach

The methodology chosen for this research is a quantitative approach which is based on a consumer survey and the previous literature review. The consumer survey examines the reaction of consumers towards appeal and price for different product types. Each product is represented with a low, mid and high tier retailer brand product as well as one branded product. The quantitative approach is based on the positivist paradigm *(Saunders, M., Lewis, P., Thornhill, A. 2009)*, which is a common base for the scientific method. The positivist paradigm requires empirical research, aims for generalization and assumes objective truth *(Saunders, M., Lewis, P., Thornhill, A. 2009)*. The aim of the study to provide general, industry-wide implications of the relation between packaging and pricing for the food segment in Germany, clearly support the use of the positivist paradigm. As stated in the research limitations a generalization outside of Germany has to be carefully evaluated given potential cultural differences, but also the limitation of four food categories only.

The research is conducted using only a quantitative research approach. Universally, this type of research should allow the generalization of findings as well as the ability to create casual relationships upon it *(Saunders, M., Lewis, P., Thornhill, A. 2009)*. The research vehicle is an online consumer survey (target is to get at least 150 valid responses) targeted to grocery purchase decision makers based in Germany (see detailed questionnaire in appendix 7.1).

3.3. Level of the research

The level of research is defined for food consumers, who reside in Germany and possess the purchase decision for their household. This level of research will help to integrate issues including consumer perception of product appeal and associated willingness to pay. It will also help to determine whether there will be any demographic factors influencing the impact.

3.4. Population and sample size

The consumer population is composed of random participants to the online survey with a target of minimum 150 valid full responses. The participants was recruited via a snowball sampling method. The researcher will leverage various internet forums to advertise the survey, however there is no direct mailing to a given distribution list involved. Whilst this form of participant recruitment is not a probabilistic method, it is sufficient to provide a random sample if the sample size is large enough *(Saunders, M., Lewis, P., Thornhill, A. 2009)*. Given the minimum sample size of 150 valid responses it is therefore appropriate in this case.

3.5. Data collection

The provider used for the survey application and server capacity is Lamapoll (http://www.lamapoll.de).

The data collection will be performed online using a survey instrument. This survey instrument is included in the Appendix (**Fehler! Verweisquelle konnte nicht gefunden werden.** original, 7.2 English translation).

The survey is structured into three main parts with different purposes. In part 1 (questions 1 to 2) the participant is evaluated in terms of eligibility to participate in the survey. In order to participate in the survey the participant needs to be a grocery purchase decision maker and live in Germany. Both is verified with respective questions: i) on where the participant lives (Drop Down menu with all countries) and ii) who is making the grocery purchase decision (multiple choice). Only if both questions are passed based on the pre-requisite (Germany and Myself) the remainder of the survey will appear, else the survey is closed.

In part 2 (questions 4 to 67) the participant will be presented four different products (retailer brand tier 3, retailer brand tier 2, retailer brand tier 1 and branded product) in four different food categories (ham, jam, ice cream and cheese). Importantly, the order of the four categories is random in each survey to avoid any potential impact by having a certain category always in the beginning/end of the survey. For each product the participant will need to provide:

- Willingness to pay – What price the participant is willing to pay for the product (scale 0,50€ to 5,00€)
- How appealing is the product – Score for the product (1 low to 6 high)
- Has the participant purchased the product before (Yes, No or No Answer)
- Only if he has purchased it, was the participant satisfied (Yes, No or No Answer)

This data will be used to determine the relationship between price and packaging perception (WTP and appeal score). Specifically, the differentials will be used i.e. the gap in price and product score of the retailer brand tier 2/3 and branded product versus the retailer brand tier 1 product. The past purchase information is collected to eliminate a potential consumer experience from the data set as it might influence the scoring and WTP. Any significant differences will be included in the data analysis.

Finally, in part 3 (questions 3 and 68 to 71) the participant is asked for five demographic data points. The first one is a self-assessment on shopping behaviour:

- Impulsive: I consider myself to be a very spontaneous shopper and often buy products that I didn't plan to. I choose the product that has good reputation, even if I pay more
- Functional: As long as the product works, I care less about the brand, more about the price
- Loyal: I normally go for products that are proven to work well and brands I trust.

The remaining four demographic questions are linked to age, gender, household size and household income. All five will be used to determine potential correlation of demographics and willingness to pay.

3.6. Data analysis

Analysis of the consumer responses will be performed using linear regression, one way analysis of variance (ANOVA) and means testing to determine the correlation of perception of quality and willingness to pay as well as the demographic drivers such as age, gender, household size and income and shopping behaviour. This analysis will be performed in SPSS 19.

3.7. Data presentation

Data will be presented using a structured approach, in which analytical results from the survey responses and figures are presented. The data presentation will include tables, charts and statistics, followed by an interpretation of results and contextualization within the existing research. This will provide context and will be used to verify the research questions and phrase possible recommendations.

3.8. Ethics

The main area of possible ethical issues identified for this research was the potential harm to individual participants due to the consumer survey. However, consumers were polled anonymously and no information was kept on their identity or location, beyond verifying a likely location in Germany through a mandatory question collected as part of the online survey (Question 2). Hence, this should not cause any ethical issue.

3.9. Reliability, validity and generalization

Reliability and validity will be discussed in the context of the statistical models that are used for the data analysis. Reliability refers to the ability of the instruments to reflect a specific construct *(Saunders, M., Lewis, P., Thornhill, A. 2009)*. Reliability for the analysis of the consumer survey will be considered in terms of credibility and information reliability. This will be discussed based on the results of the analysis tools used, such as a linear regression.

Validity indicates the ability to transfer the findings to the real-world conditions *(Saunders, M., Lewis, P., Thornhill, A. 2009)*. The literature divides validity into criterion, concurrent and predictive validity *(Saunders, M., Lewis, P., Thornhill, A. 2009)*. The criterion and concurrent validity will be addressed in the analysis in the form of e.g. ANOVA and chi-square tests in addition to the linear regression. However, the predictive validity cannot be measured at this time given that it would require an extensive waiting period (for example sales data after one year with initial packaging rating) which is beyond the scope of this study. The targeted size of the consumer sample (n = >150 valid answers), should allow for generalization of the data. Any data points from the survey indicating the opposite, i.e. a potential conflict in generalization will be discussed in the results.

4. Quantitative analysis results and discussion

4.1. Arrangement of the chapter

This chapter presents the statistical results and analysis of the survey conducted (Appendix 7.1). The statistical analysis is intended to answer three specific research questions, as laid out in chapter 1.5:

1. Are consumers willing to pay a price premium for retailer brand Tier 1 products compared to branded and retailer brands Tier 2 / Tier 3 products based on the packaging appeal?
2. Do current retailer brand tier 1 premium priced products justify their price premium based on the packaging impression?
3. Are there demographic specifications such as gender, age, household size, household income or shopping behaviour influencing the willingness to pay a premium price?

First, a profile of the participants is presented to show the characteristics of the survey sample. This is followed by a brief description of the analysis strategy. Subsequently, four sections present a quantitative analysis for each of the four grocery categories. The final section summarizes the findings and provides a conclusive answer to each of the research questions based on these findings.

4.2. Participants profile

The intent of the survey was to reach at least 150 valid responses, which has been achieved with n = 159 valid responses. In total 273 replies were collected. However 42 surveys have been stopped as participants did not meet either the requirements i) of living in Germany or ii) being the grocery purchase decision maker as asked in question 1 and question 2. Out of the 231 eligible participants 72 aborted the survey at any point, whilst 159 successfully completed all questions. Given 159 represents a meaningful sample the entire analysis of responses will only take into account these 159 fully completed surveys.

Figure 5: Distribution of survey replies

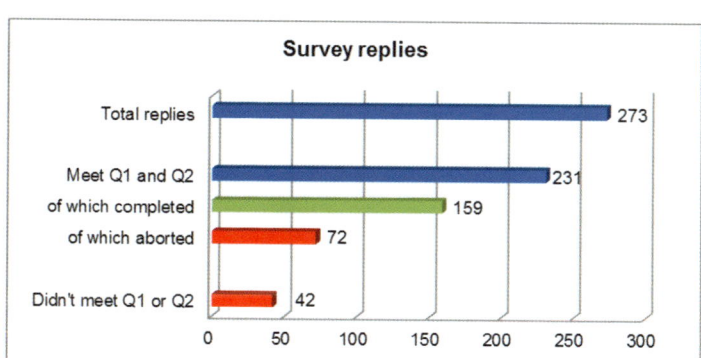

As part of the survey five shopper characteristics were collected, to cluster participants according to demographics. These include gender, age, income range, household size and shopper behaviour (a self-descriptive category).

The gender split is close to be even between female (n = 72, 45%) and male (n = 87, 55%). Although a uniform distribution would be expected, a chi-square test ($\chi2$ = 1,415, p = 0,234) did not show a significant difference in distribution given p > 0,05. Thus, despite not being uniform the gender distribution is acceptable for the survey.

Figure 6: Gender distribution in the sample

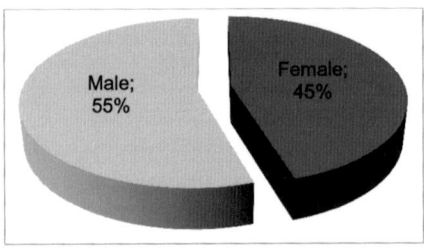

Figure 7 shows the age distribution of the survey. Results indicate that the largest group of respondents is aged 30 to 49 years (47%), while the smallest group is aged over 50 years (23%). This is not necessarily as expected, but could be due to the data collection method, which would privilege younger, more technologically comfortable users that spend more time online. However, the youngest age group 18 to 29 years is still only the second highest (30%). Hence, the age distribution remains a watch-out for the generalization of results, especially if age becomes a driver of differences in findings, but overall can be judged as acceptable

Figure 7: Age distribution in the sample

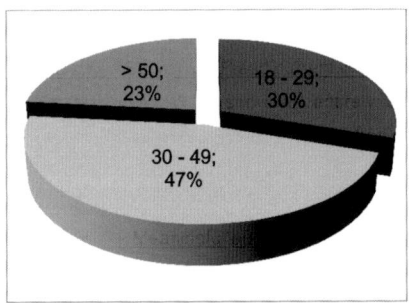

Figure 8 shows the monthly net income distribution, indicating that the highest reported income category is 1000 to 3000 Euro (50% of the sample). This is very much in line with the average monthly net income in Germany, which is according to *Statistisches Bundesamt (2013)* gross 3391 Euro monthly resulting in a respective net income of 60-70% of that, i.e. 2035 to 2374 Euro. This suggests that the average net income of respondents is representing the country average. However, 11% of the sample did not answer this question, which could alter the results slightly.

Figure 8: Net income distribution in the sample

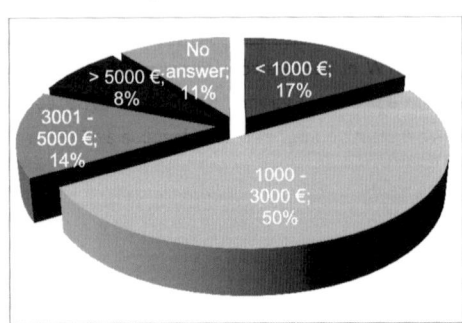

The household size was the final demographic question collected from the sample. Possible answers for the household size ranged from 1 to 5 members. For the later results review, households are classified as single (1 person), couple (2 people), or family (3+ people). The average household size (Mean = 2,04) in the survey as well as the % distribution as shown in Figure 9 is consistent with the German average according to *Statistisches Bundesamt (2013b)* and as such the sample is representative.

Figure 9: Household size distribution in the sample

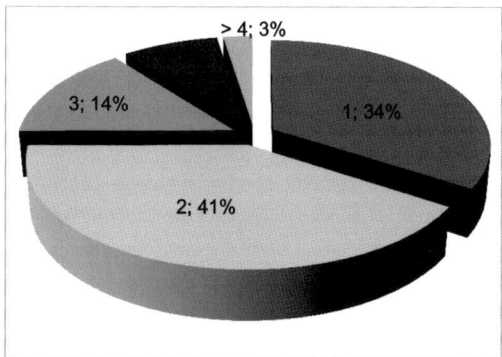

In addition, a single psychographic question was collected. This question asked shoppers to characterize their shopping behaviour as loyal, functional, or impulsive based on a descriptive statement as descried in chapter 3.5. Figure 10 summarizes the distribution of these responses. This shows that the most frequently selected self-descriptor was functional (47%), while the least frequently selected was Impulsive (23%).

Figure 10: Shopping behaviour distribution in the sample

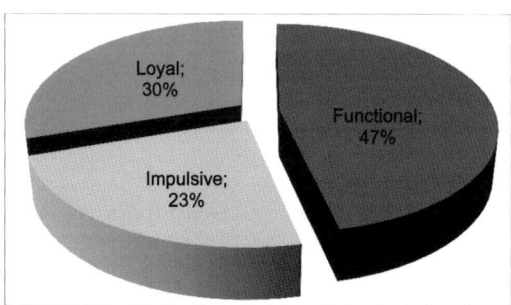

4.3. Analysis strategy

In the following four sections each of the four grocery categories is assessed leveraging the same analysis strategy. First, a general set of descriptive statistics is presented in order to show the overall reactions to the products, including willingness to pay (price) and packaging score as well as whether or not consumers purchased them in the past and if so liked them. To answer research question 1, a single linear regression is used with the predictor variable being the difference in packaging score between the retailer brand tier 1 product and the compared product and the outcome variable being the price premium (difference of willingness to pay between the retailer brand tier 1 product and the respective other product). This test is repeated for each pair of categories (Tier 1 vs. Tier 2, Tier 3 and Branded). To answer research question 2, a single linear regression is used, with the packaging score being the predictor variable and the price consumers are willing to pay for the premium brand being the outcome variable. To answer research question 3, a one-way ANOVA test is used for each of the demographic and psychographic categories.

4.4. Analysis of survey results for ham

For the ham category the survey had embedded four different products currently in market. Notably, as shown in Figure 11 the retailer brand Tier 1 product currently in market has a substantial price premium of 207% versus the branded product and 272% versus the retailer brand Tier 2 product (per 100gr comparison). As such it represents a true premium product.

Figure 11: Overview of ham products included in the survey

Ham products included in the survey					
	Product	Price €	Price € per 100ml/gr	Price premium Tier 1 vs. product €	Price premium Tier 1 vs. product %
Tier 1 - Feine Welt	Rewe Feine Welt Kochschinken	4,69	4,69	-	-
Branded Product	Herta Finesse Schinken	2,29	1,53	3,16	207%
Tier 2 - REWE	Rewe Delikatess Metzgerschinken	1,89	1,26	3,43	272%
Tier 3 - ja!	Ja! Delikatess Kochschinken	1,29	0,65	4,05	627%
All prices based on http://www.rewe.de on 26th February 2013, excluding any special promotion prices					

4.4.1. Descriptive statistics for ham

Figure 12 through Figure 13 show the descriptive statistics for the willingness to pay (WTP), packaging scores as well as previous purchase frequency for ham for each of the products tested. Figure 12 shows that the mean for retailer Tier 1 WTP is higher than all other WTP indications. As expected, Tier 1 ham possesses a price premium compared to all other products. Remarkably, this is also the case versus the respective branded product, however versus both Tier 2 and the branded product the indicated premium is only within a range of a few cents. This also does not mirror the current in-store picture, which shows a significant price premium for the Tier 1 product. In contrast branded ham has the highest packaging score, followed by Tier 2 ham. This indicates an interesting disconnect from packaging scores and WTP, as not the highest scored product achieves the highest WTP. Importantly, the standard deviation across products and across WTP and packaging means is fairly equal across products, leading to the conclusion that the range and variation of WTP and packaging scores across products is pretty similar.

Figure 13 shows that participants have most frequently purchased Tier 3 ham, whilst Tier 1 ham is least frequently purchased.

Figure 12: Willingness to pay and packaging scores for ham

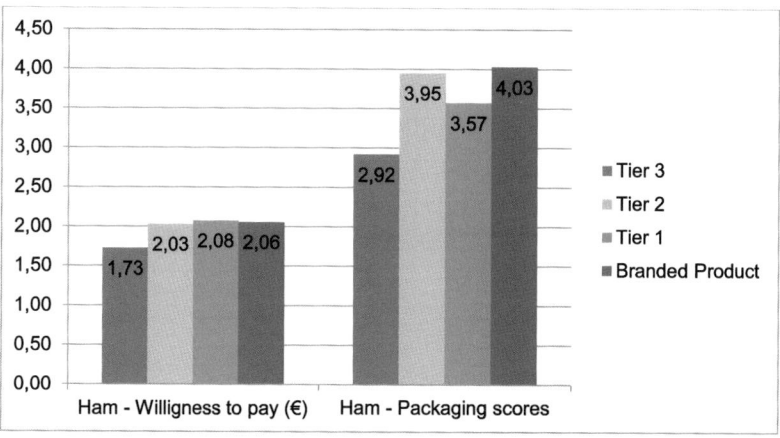

Figure 13: Previous purchase for ham

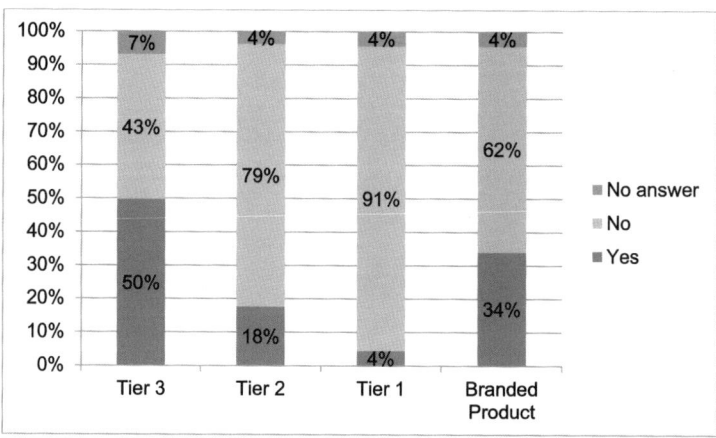

4.4.2. Exploration of research questions for ham

The first research question addresses whether the packaging score justifies the price premium of the Tier 1 product versus each of the products. Figure 14 summarizes the outcomes of the linear regression between the difference in packaging score (predictor variable) and price premium (outcome variable) for each of the three other products. Overall, the results are mixed as the amount of explained variation varies between 13% (Tier 2 product adj. R2 = 0,127) and 20% (Branded product adj. R2 = 0,203). With 20% the amount of explained variation starts to become meaningful, but is yet at rather at the low end. However, as the ANOVA test confirms all results are statistically significant. Hence, there is an indication that at least for the branded product and retailer brand Tier 3 product the packaging has an influence on the price premium a consumer is willing to pay.

The regression outcome changes slightly when excluding all participants who have purchased either of the compared products in the past to avoid any influence from the product experience. Whilst the change for the branded adj. R2 is minor, the R2 for Tier 3 drops by -0,06 whilst the R2 for Tier 2 increases by +0,06. The details are summarized in Appendix 7.1, Figure 62. Hence, there is no clear indication that previous purchases influence the package appeal or price perception.

Figure 14: Summary of regression outcomes for packaging and price premium for ham

Summary ham regression analysis (packaging/price premium)			
Tier 1 vs.	Retailer Brand		Branded
	Tier 3	Tier 2	Product
Model Summary			
R2	0,199	0,132	0,208
Adjusted R2	0,194	0,127	0,203
ANOVA			
F (sig)	39,046 (p = ,000)	23,952 (p = ,000)	41,245 (p = ,000)
Coefficients			
Unstandardized Beta	0,176	0,139	0,16
Standardized Beta	0,446	0,364	0,456
T (sig)	6,249 (p = ,000)	4,894 (p = ,000)	6,422 (p = ,000)

Figure 15 summarizes the linear regression test for the second research question, which addresses the impact of packaging score on WTP. The outcome of this test shows a very low r-squared value (adj. R2 = 0,042). The test is shown to be significant by the ANOVA outcome (F = 7,966, p = 0,005), but the predictive value is very low (4%) based on the adj. R2 score. Overall, this test does not support the idea that there is a relationship between the packaging score and the WTP for the retailer's Tier 1 packaged ham product. There is no difference in results by excluding previous buyers of the Tier 1 product, given these account only for 4% of the total participants. The same is true for the third research question.

Figure 15: Summary of regression outcomes for packaging and willingness to pay for ham

Summary ham regression analysis (packaging/willigness to pay)	
Retailer Brand Tier 1	
Model Summary	
R2	0,048
Adjusted R2	0,042
ANOVA	
F (sig)	7,966 (p = ,005)
Coefficients	
Unstandardized Beta	0,101
Standardized Beta	0,22
T (sig)	2,822 (p = ,005)

The final research question is whether consumer demographic characteristics influence the WTP for the Tier 1 ham product. Figure 16 summarizes the results from the ANOVA tests used to evaluate this question. This shows that there were significant means differences in age and household size. The shopper profile is just very slightly above the significance level of 0,05 . LSD and Bonferroni tests were used to determine the significant mean differences for age and household size. For Age, the 18-29 years group had a significantly lower price they were willing to pay than the over 50 years group (mean difference -0,276, p = 0,048). For the household size category, the family group (3 or more members) was significantly less WTP for premium ham than either the single (means difference = -0,288, p = 0,031) or couple (means difference = -0,355, p = 0,006) groups.

Figure 16: Impact of demographics on willingness to pay for Tier 1 ham (ANOVA results)

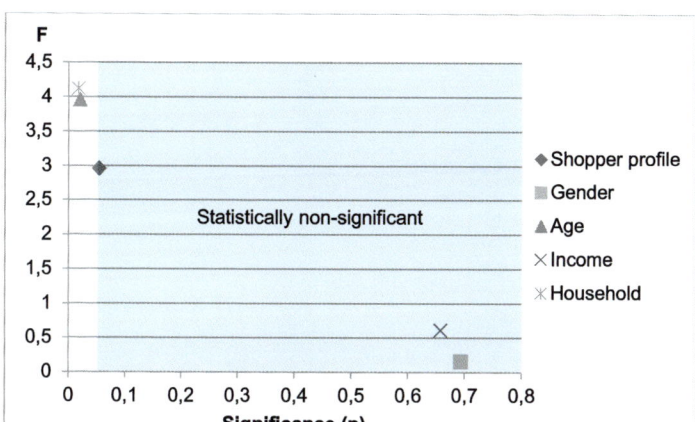

4.4.3. Conclusions from analysis of the ham survey results

Based on the analysis it can be concluded that the research questions have been only partly proofed within the ham category.

Descriptive statistics - Survey WTP and current in-store price premium strongly differ

The overall mean WTP showed a significant difference versus the current in-store price premiums. Further, the survey results only indicate a low difference in WTP, whilst the mean packaging scores strongly varied.

Research question 1 – Meaningful amount of variance explained versus branded and Tier 3 product

The results were significant, but mixed in terms of showing a high explanation of the variation of difference of packaging score and price. The amount of WTP variance explained by packaging is overall low, and only meaningful for the branded and Tier 3 product (20% of variance explained).

Research question 2 – No relationship between packaging score and WTP for Tier 1 product

It has been clearly shown that differences in packaging perception scores do not influence WTP for the Tier 1 ham product as only 4% of the variation is explained by this relationship.

Research question 3 – Age and household size impact WTP for the Tier 1 ham product

There were statistical significant results for age and household size related to the WTP for the Tier 1 product based on the one-way ANOVA tests. The post hoc analysis showed that the oldest group had a higher mean WTP than the youngest group. Similarly, single or couple household had a higher WTP than families (household size 3+).

4.5. Analysis of survey results for cheese

The second grocery category to be examined is cheese. As shown in Figure 17 the retailer brand Tier 1 price premium is 179% versus the respective branded product, again representing a true premium product. Remarkably, also the absolute in-store price point of 3,99€ is by far the highest confirming this positioning.

Figure 17: Overview of cheese products included in the survey

	Product	Price €	Price € per 100ml/gr	Price premium Tier 1 vs. product €	Price premium Tier 1 vs. product %
Tier 1 - Feine Welt	Rewe Feine Welt Fleur de Biere	3,99	2,00	-	-
Branded Product	Champignon Camembert	1,39	1,11	0,88	79%
Tier 2 - REWE	Rewe Weichkäse	0,75	0,75	1,25	166%
Tier 3 - ja!	Ja! Camembert	0,59	0,47	1,52	323%

All prices based on http://w w w .rew e.de on 26th February 2013, excluding any special promotion prices

4.5.1. Descriptive statistics for cheese

Figure 18 shows again that the retailer brand Tier 1 product has the highest WTP results and hence possesses a price premium over other tiers, with the highest premium being versus Tier 3. However, the price premium resulting from the survey is far less than the current in-store positioning, e.g. versus the branded product the survey results a WTP gap of +7% compared to +79% in-store. Packaging scores in the same figure show that the highest average packaging score was found for the Tier 1 products. Therefore packaging appeal and price premium are synchronized in the cheese category, i.e. highest price has the highest packaging score. The standard deviation across WTP and packaging scores is very similar, with the only exception being the retailer brand Tier 2 product which has a slightly lower deviation. However, also for cheese the variation of scores for WTP and packaging is very similar across products. Finally, Figure 19 shows the frequency of purchase for each product. This shows that the most common cheese purchased is the branded cheese, with the retailer brand Tier 1 cheese hardly being purchased so far.

Figure 18: Willingness to pay and packaging scores for cheese

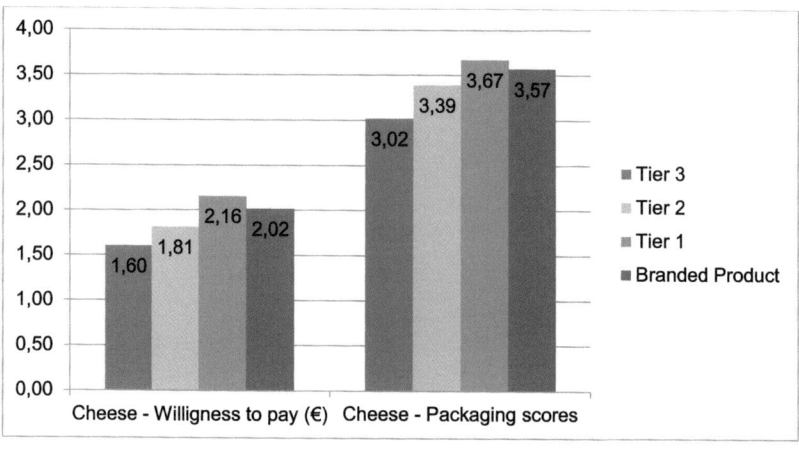

Figure 19: Previous purchase for cheese

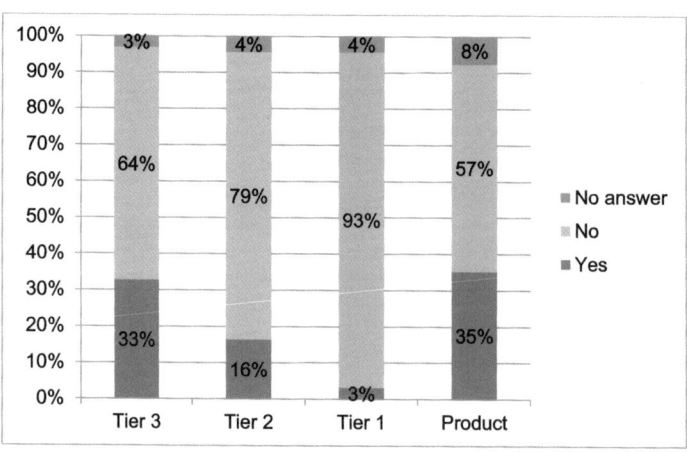

4.5.2. Exploration of research questions for cheese

The first research question asks whether the difference in product scores justify the difference in WTP (price premium) between the product tiers. Figure 20 summarizes the outcomes of the regression tests to deal with this question. As this shows, all results are statistically significant. However, the predictive power (R^2) of difference in packaging scores on price premiums is low enough to be practically insignificant. The highest level is 15% of explanation in variance comparing the retailer brand Tier 1 product versus the retailer brand Tier 3 and branded product. Based on these findings the answer to research question 1 for cheese products is that there is no practical impact of differences in packaging attractiveness on price premiums over different products.

The exclusion or participants who purchased the products previously does not drive a change of this finding. Whilst results for Tier 3 and branded differ slightly by 1-3%, the change on Tier 2 is +6%. Hence, across Tiers the R2 value remains low (<15%) and hence rather insignificant (summary in Appendix 7.1, Figure 62).

Figure 20: Summary of regression outcomes for packaging and price premium for cheese

Summary cheese regression analysis (packaging/price premium)			
Tier 1 vs.	Retailer Brand		Branded
	Tier 3	Tier 2	Product
Model Summary			
R2	0,157	0,062	0,155
Adjusted R2	0,151	0,056	0,150
ANOVA			
F (sig)	29,134 (p = ,000)	10,310 (p = ,002)	28,889 (p = ,000)
Coefficients			
Unstandardized Beta	0,202	0,11	0,172
Standardized Beta	0,396	0,248	0,394
T (sig)	5,398 (p = ,000)	3,211 (p = ,002)	5,375 (p = ,000)

The second research question asks whether packaging attractiveness has an influence on WTP for the product. As Figure 21 shows, the results are statistically significant as indicated by the ANOVA test, but practically unimportant. With an adjusted R2 of only 0,089, this means that only 8.9% of the variance in estimated WTP can be explained by the packaging attractiveness score. Based on these findings, the answer to research question 2 for this product is that there is no impact of packaging attractiveness on WTP. There is no difference in results by excluding previous buyers of the Tier 1 product, given these account only for 3% of the total participants. The same is true for the third research question.

Figure 21: Summary of regression outcomes for packaging and willingness to pay for cheese

Summary cheese regression analysis (packaging/willigness to pay	
	Retailer Brand Tier 1
Model Summary	
R2	0,095
Adjusted R2	0,089
ANOVA	
F (sig)	16,447 (p = ,000)
Coefficients	
Unstandardized Beta	0,159
Standardized Beta	0,308
T (sig)	4,056 (p = ,000)

The third research question asks about differences in WTP for Tier 1 cheese based on demographic categories. The results of this test are shown in Figure 22. This shows that there are no significant differences in groups based on age, gender or household size. However, there were some significant differences that were found based on household net income and the shopper profile. For shopper profile, the functional group had a lower WTP than the loyal group (mean difference = -,279, p = ,030). There were no significant differences found for the Impulsive group. For the household net income, those with an income of less than 1,000 Euros a month had a lower WTP than those with an income of 3000 to

5000 Euro per month (mean difference = -,530, p = ,008). Those with an income of 1000 to 3000 Euro per month also had a lower WTP than those with 3000 to 5000 Euro per month (mean difference = -,551, p = ,001). Interestingly, the highest income category of >5000 Euro did not show any similar significant result. This might be driven by the small sample size of only 13 replies. Generally, the WTP for a retailer brand Tier 1 product is strongly driven by the middle to high income category. Based on the above findings, the answer to research question 3 is that there is a significant difference in shopper Profile behind the loyal shoppers and household net income behind the middle to high income group, but not behind other demographic categories.

Figure 22: Impact of demographics on willingness to pay for Tier 1 cheese (ANOVA results)

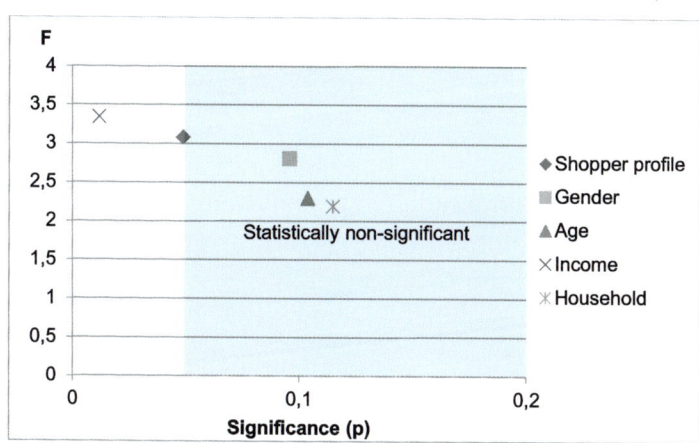

4.5.3. Conclusions from analysis of the cheese survey results

Based on the findings only the hypothesis of the third research question, demographics drive WTP for Tier 1 products, could be proven for the cheese category.

Descriptive statistics - Survey WTP and current in-store price premiums strongly differ

The Tier 1 product scored highest in packaging appeal and WTP, but the mean WTP across products does not confirm the current in-store price premiums

Research question 1 – No meaningful explanation of variation in WTP by packaging appeal

With the highest predictive score of 15% for Tier 3 and branded products there is no proven meaningful relationship in the cheese category between differences in packaging appeal and WTP.

Research question 2 – No relationship between packaging score and WTP for Tier 1 product

Only 9% of the variance in WTP for Tier 1 is driven behind the packaging appeal, hence there is no meaningful relationship.

Research question 3 – Shopper profile and household income impact WTP for the Tier 1 cheese product

There are differences in WTP for retailer brand Tier 1 cheese based on demographic categories including household income and shopper profile. Those indicate that middle to high income groups as well as loyal shoppers are tending to show a higher WTP.

4.6. Analysis of survey results for jam

The jam products used in the survey show very similar pricing differences as the previous categories, with the retailer brand Tier 1 product having a true price premium of 132% versus the branded product and 182%/289% versus retailer brand Tier 2/Tier3 products. However, the absolute price point leader is the branded product in this case, primarily driven by the available size.

Figure 23: Overview of jam products included in the survey

	Product	Price €	Price € per 100ml/gr	Price premium Tier 1 vs. product €	Price premium Tier 1 vs. product %
Tier 1 - Feine Welt	Rewe Feine Welt Sonnige Erdbeere	1,59	0,64	-	-
Branded Product	Schwartau Extra Erdbeermarmelade	2,89	0,48	0,15	32%
Tier 2 - REWE	Rewe Erdbeermarmelade	1,19	0,35	0,29	82%
Tier 3 - ja!	Ja! Erdbeermarmelade	0,99	0,22	0,42	189%

All prices based on http://www.rewe.de on 26th February 2013, excluding any special promotion prices

4.6.1. Descriptive statistics for jam

Figure 24 through Figure 25 show the descriptive statistics for the jam category similar to the previous categories. As indicated in Figure 24 the highest WTP is for the branded jam product, whilst Tier 2 and Tier 1 products are fairly equal below. Therefore the highest price premium for the Tier 1 product is versus Tier 3, whilst it is actually negative (-0,12) versus the branded product. This sets the jam category apart from ham and cheese, where the highest WTP was for the retailer Tier 1 product. Also this is a significant contradiction to the current in-store price positioning which shows a 32% price premium of Tier 1 versus the branded product and 82% versus the Tier 2 product. However the jam packaging scores for the four categories underpin these results. Figure 24 also shows that the branded product has the most attractive package, followed by the retailer brand Tier 2 jam. Tier 1 jam only ranks third. Hence, the packaging scores not fully confirm the WTP ranking. Again, the standard deviation across products and means is very similar and does not indicate a substantial difference. Finally, Figure 25 shows that the most frequently purchased jam is the branded jam, followed by the Tier 3 jam. Tier 1 jam, like ham and cheese, is the least frequently purchased.

Figure 24: Willingness to pay and packaging scores for jam

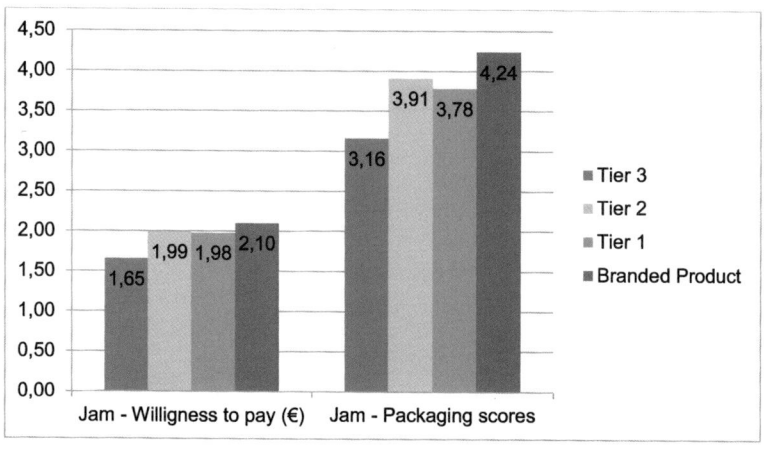

Figure 25: Previous purchase for jam

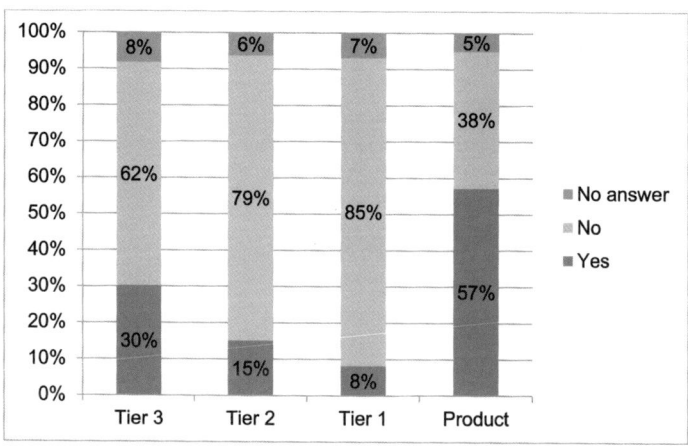

4.6.2. Exploration of research questions for jam

Figure 26 shows the regression outcome for research question 1 (the relationship between difference in packaging scores and price premiums). The results indicate a strong relationship as R2 is > 20% for all products, with Tier 3 even indicating 35%. This indicates that a sufficient amount of the variance in price premium can be explained by the difference in packaging score. All results are confirmed to be statistically significant by the ANOVA test.

Excluding the participants who have purchased the products in the past (Summary in Appendix 7.1, Figure 62) the results for Tier 2/3 drop slightly -2%/-4%, however remain significant. The key change is the result of the regression of the branded product versus the Tier 1 product. The R2 drops significantly by -0,16 resulting in a low 5,2% variance explanation. However, the results could be explained by the strongly reduced amount of responses n = 57 compared to the n = 159 in the total survey. The branded product has been purchased by nearly 2/3 of participants. Therefore it remains a watchout item if the finding for branded can be easily generalized.

Figure 26: Summary of regression outcomes for packaging and price premium for jam

Summary jam regression analysis (packaging/price premium)			
Tier 1 vs.	Retailer Brand		Branded
	Tier 3	Tier 2	Product
Model Summary			
R2	0,350	0,207	0,215
Adjusted R2	0,345	0,202	0,210
ANOVA			
F (sig)	84,367 (p = ,000)	40,985 (p = ,000)	43,033 (p = ,000)
Coefficients			
Unstandardized Beta	0,215	0,192	0,179
Standardized Beta	0,591	0,455	0,464
T (sig)	9,185 (p = ,000)	6,402 (p = ,000)	6,560 (p = ,000)

Results for research question 2 (the relationship between packaging and price premium) are shown in Figure 27. These results are very weak by comparison, with only 6% of variation in WTP being explained by variation in packaging appeal score. This result can be characterized as statistically significant, but not relevant in terms of great practical importance. There is no difference in results by excluding previous buyers of the Tier 1 product, given these account only for 8% of the total participants. The same is true for the third research question.

Figure 27: Summary of regression outcomes for packaging and willingness to pay for jam

Summary jam regression analysis (packaging/willigness to pay)	
	Retailer Brand Tier 1
Model Summary	
R2	0,066
Adjusted R2	0,06
ANOVA	
F (sig)	11,158 (p = ,001)
Coefficients	
Unstandardized Beta	0,132
Standardized Beta	0,258
T (sig)	3,340 (p = ,001)

The third research question addresses demographic differences in WTP. In this case, gender, age, and income did not show significant differences (though income approaches significance at p = ,058). However, shopper profile and household size show some significant differences in price. As with the cheese category, loyal shoppers had a higher WTP than functional shoppers (mean difference = ,313, p = ,008). Similarly, family households (those with three or more family members) had a higher WTP than single shoppers (mean difference = ,326, p = ,015). This suggests that there are significant differences in the WTP of shoppers for jam products based on shopper profile (loyal) and household size (families).

Figure 28: Impact of demographics on willingness to pay for Tier 1 jam (ANOVA results)

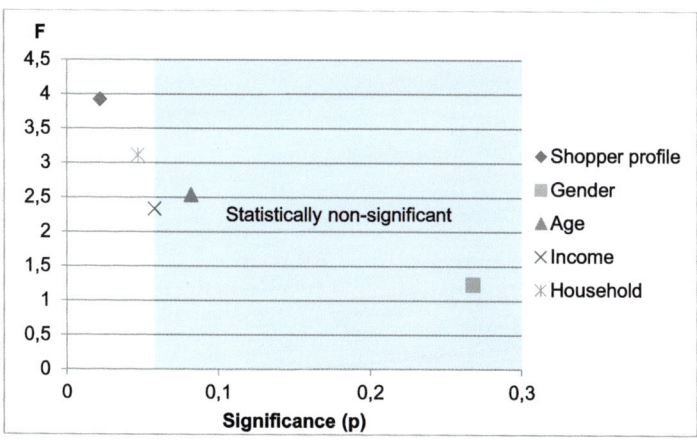

4.6.3. Conclusions from analysis of the jam survey results

The jam category results confirm an overall strong meaningful relationship of WTP and packaging appeal across products, as well as a higher WTP by loyal buyers and families for the Tier 1 product.

Descriptive statistics - Survey WTP and current in-store price points strongly differ

The results of the mean WTP show an entirely different outcome than the current in-store price premiums, given the retailer brand Tier 1 product only ranks third in absolute WTP and also packaging appeal.

Research question 1 – Meaningful amount of variance in WTP explained by packaging appeal

There is a strong relationship between difference in packaging appeal and price premium with up to 35% of variance explained. Importantly, the jam category is so far the only category where the exclusion of participants with a previous purchase drives a significant change in results (Tier 1 vs. branded variance explanation dropped from 21% to 5%). Hence, whilst this might be driven by the low amount of participants left, the proof of a relationship cannot be easily generalized for all products in the category.

Research question 2 – No relationship between packaging score and WTP for Tier 1 jam

The relationship between packaging attractiveness and WTP for Tier 1 products is very weak and does not confirm the hypothesis.

Research question 3 – Shopper profile and household size impact WTP for the Tier 1 jam product

There are some demographic differences in WTP, including the shopper profile and household size categories. Loyal buyers and families (3+ members) have a statistically significant tendency to have a higher WTP. This suggests that demographic factors play a partial role in WTP for jam.

4.7. Analysis of survey results for ice cream

The final category of grocery products is ice cream. The four products chosen for the ice cream category as shown in Figure 29 indicate the lowest in-store price premium difference between the retailer brand Tier 1 product and the branded product with 20%. Still, the price premium versus the other retailer brand tiers is substantial with 116%/421%. However, the highest absolute price point is owned by the branded product, driven by the size.

Figure 29: Overview of ice cream products included in the survey

	Product	Price €	Price € per 100ml/gr	Price premium Tier 1 vs. product €	Price premium Tier 1 vs. product %
	Ice cream products included in the survey				
Tier 1 - Feine Welt	Rewe Feine Welt Pures Vergnügen	2,29	0,48	-	-
Branded Product	Mövenpick Eis Bourbon Vanille	3,59	0,40	0,08	20%
Tier 2 - REWE	Rewe Eis Bourbon Vanille	1,99	0,22	0,26	116%
Tier 3 - ja!	Ja! Eiskrem Bourbon Vanille	2,29	0,09	0,39	421%

All prices based on http://www.rewe.de on 26th February 2013, excluding any special promotion prices

4.7.1. Descriptive statistics for ice cream

Figure 30 shows that, like in the jam category, the mean WTP for the branded product is highest, followed by the retailer Tier 1 price. Hence, the price premiums between Tier 1 ice cream and the other products indicate a slight premium versus Tier 2, but actually a strong negative premium versus the branded product (-0,32). The mean WTP results also don't reflect the current in-store price premiums. Packaging appeal scores indicate that the branded product has the most attractive packaging, followed by retailer brand Tier 1, Tier 2 and Tier 3. Similar to all other categories before the standard deviation is very close for all products and WTP and packaging score mean results. Finally, Figure 31 shows the purchase frequency associated with these products. This shows that the branded ice cream is the most frequently purchased, whilst Tier 1 ice cream is the least frequently purchased.

Figure 30: Willingness to pay and packaging scores for ice cream

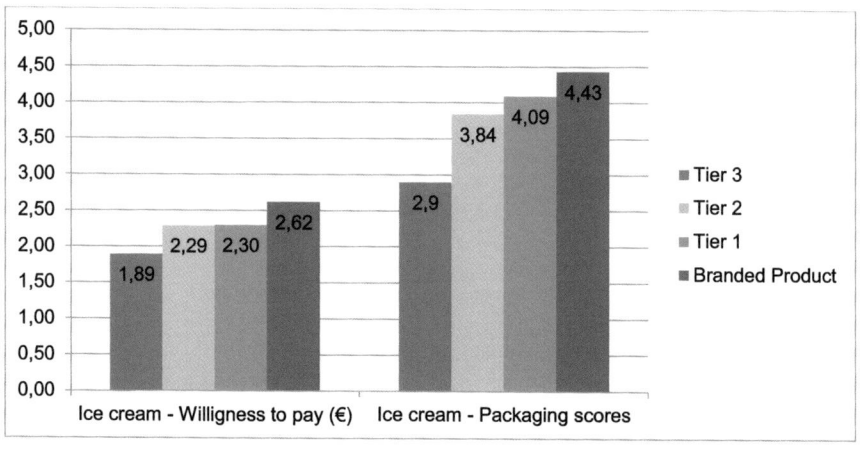

Figure 31: Previous purchase for ice cream

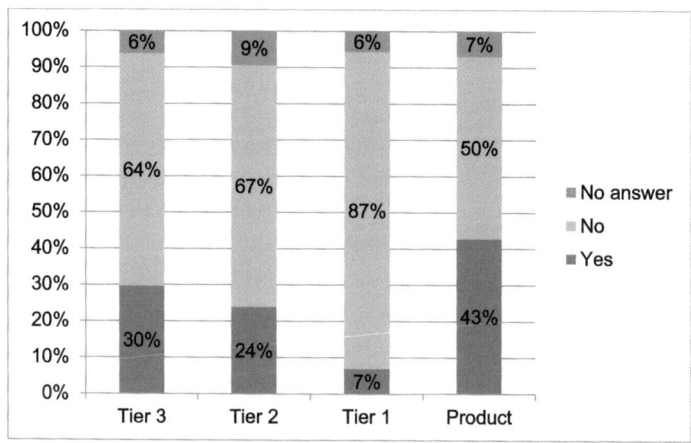

4.7.2. Exploration of research questions for ice cream

The results of the regression test confirm the hypothesis of research question 1 (the impact of difference in packaging attractiveness on price premiums) as shown in Figure 32. The strongest adjusted R2 score results from the relationship between retailer brand Tier 1 and Tier 3 with 28%. This is closely followed by Tier 2 with 25%, however the branded product scores very low at 12% of variance explained. The results are therefore mixed as the relationship of difference in packaging and WTP for Tier 1 versus Tier 2/ Tier 3 explains a sufficient amount of the variance, but not for the branded product. Importantly, all results are statistically significant as shown by the ANOVA test.

Importantly, these findings change when excluding all previous participants with a previous purchase and hence a potential influence by the product experience (summary table in Appendix 7.1, Figure 62). Whilst still statistically significant, all R2 values drop by up to -0,16. The highest variance explained is now 18% (Tier 1 vs. Tier 2), whilst Tier 3 (13%) and Branded product (8%) are fairly low. Therefore the ice cream category results are mixed and hence potentially influenced by past purchase experiences or potentially as well the low amount of remaining participants given the high amount of previous purchases.

Figure 32: Summary of regression outcomes for packaging and price premium for ice cream

Summary ice cream regression analysis (packaging/price premium)			
Tier 1 vs.	Retailer Brand		Branded
	Tier 3	Tier 2	Product
Model Summary			
R2	0,288	0,252	0,124
Adjusted R2	0,284	0,248	0,119
ANOVA			
F (sig)	63,526 (p = ,000)	52,999 (p = ,000)	22,319 (p = ,000)
Coefficients			
Unstandardized Beta	0,250	0,246	0,164
Standardized Beta	0,537	0,502	0,353
T (sig)	7,970 (p = ,000)	7,280 (p = ,000)	4,724 (p = ,000)

The outcome of the regression test for research question 2 (the relationship between packaging attractiveness score and WTP) is shown in Figure 33. This shows that although once again statistically significant, the results are actually very weak, with a maximum of 5% of the variation in WTP being explained by the packaging score. Thus, although this result is statistically relevant, it may not be relevant for practical purposes such as driving sales. There is no difference in results by excluding previous buyers of the Tier 1 product, given these account only for 7% of the total participants. The same is true for the third research question.

Figure 33: Summary of regression outcomes for packaging and willingness to pay for ice cream

Summary ice cream regression analysis (packaging/willigness to pay)	
	Retailer Brand Tier 1
Model Summary	
R2	0,056
Adjusted R2	0,05
ANOVA	
F (sig)	9,388 (p = ,003)
Coefficients	
Unstandardized Beta	0,149
Standardized Beta	0,238
T (sig)	3,064 (p = ,003)

The third research question addresses demographic differences in WTP for Tier 1 ice cream.
Figure 34 summarizes the outcomes of ANOVA tests used to examine these differences. This shows that most groups, including gender, age, income and household size, do not show any significant difference in WTP for Tier 1 ice cream. However, there is a statistically significant difference derived based on the shopper profile, which is the same difference as seen in the cheese and jam categories. Specifically, there was a higher WTP on average for the loyal shopper than for the functional shopper (mean difference = ,347, p = ,007). This suggests that once again, there is an increased WTP by loyal shoppers, whilst the other demographic factors drive no statistically significant difference.

Figure 34: Impact of demographics on willingness to pay for Tier 1 ice cream (ANOVA results)

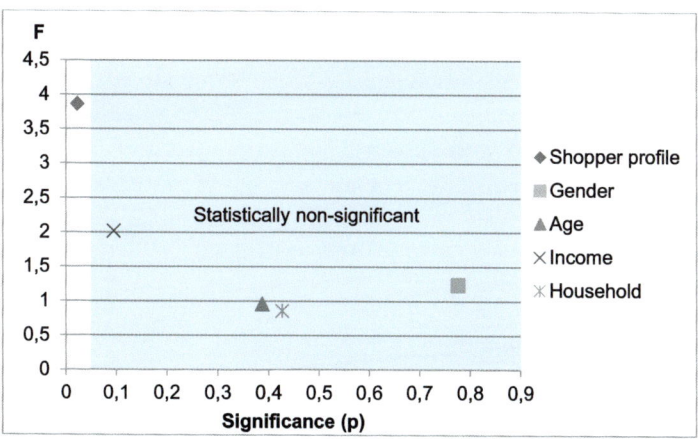

4.7.3. Conclusions from analysis of the ice cream survey results

The ice cream category results reflect a meaningful explanation of variance in WTP (across all products if previous buyers are excluded) by the packaging appeal, as well as confirm the hypothesis of demographics influencing WTP.

Descriptive statistics - Survey WTP and current in-store price points strongly differ

Also in the ice cream category the survey mean results for WTP do not reflect the in-store price premiums. The branded product WTP and packaging scores are by far the highest.

Research question 1 – Meaningful amount of variance explained versus Tier 2 and Tier 3 product

Only between the retailer brand Tier 1 and Tier 2/3 products a meaningful relationship of explaining the price premium by the difference in packaging scores can be concluded. However, results turn non-meaningful if excluding previous buyers, it is therefore not clear that these results are not influenced by previous product experience such as taste.

Research question 2 – No relationship between packaging score and WTP for Tier 1 ice cream

The relationship between packaging and WTP was one of the weakest across all categories and hence is not meaningful similar to the other categories.

Research question 3 – Shopper profile impacts WTP for the Tier 1 ice cream product

The results indicate that there is only a meaningful difference in WTP driven by the shopper profile. Similar to other categories the loyal shopper indicates a higher WTP compared to the other. Again, it confirms that demographic factors play a role in WTP.

4.8. Result summary and overall conclusions

<u>Survey Tier 1 WTP premiums are significantly lower than current in market price premiums</u>

The first key observation from comparing the mean WTP results and the current in-store prices is a significant difference in the price premium as shown in Figure 35. This suggests that there must be i) other drivers supporting the current in-store price premium (e.g. it is not a perceived price premium as the Tier 1 product might have lower volume as seen for jam and ice cream) and/or ii) the tier 1 product is very targeted on a specific consumer segment. The latter is probed with the third research question.

Figure 35: Comparison of price premium in-store and mean survey results

Price premium in % Tier 1 vs.	Ham		Cheese		Jam		Ice cream	
	In store	Mean result	In store	Mean result	In store	Mean result	In store	Mean result
Branded Product	207%	1%	79%	7%	32%	-6%	20%	-12%
Tier 2	272%	2%	166%	19%	82%	-1%	116%	1%
Tier 3	627%	20%	323%	35%	189%	20%	421%	22%

The summary of the results with regards to the research questions are summarized in Figure 36 below. As this figure shows, all of the regression results were statistically significant, but the level of predictability differs by research question. Importantly, the table shows for research question 1 the results including all participants. As the analysis has shown especially the ice-cream category (across all products) as well as the jam category (branded product) are differing if excluding participants with a previous purchase (See Figure 62 Appendix 7.1 for differences). Neither for research question 2 nor 3 the exclusion of previous purchases drives any change in results.

Figure 36: Summary of research questions analysis results

	Question 1 Packaging and price premium regression		Question 2 Packaging and willingess to pay regression		Question 3 Demographic differences in willigness to pay
	Significant	*Variation explained*	*Significant*	*Variation explained*	*Remarkable drivers*
Ham	Yes	vs. Tier 3: 19,4% vs. Tier 2: 12,7% vs. Brand: 20,3%	Yes	4,2%	household size, age, shopper profile (slightly above p = 0,05)
Cheese	Yes	vs. Tier 3: 15,1% vs. Tier 2: 5,6% vs. Brand: 15,0%	Yes	8,9%	shopper profile, income
Jam	Yes	vs. Tier 3: 34,5% vs. Tier 2: 20,2% vs. Brand: 21,0%	Yes	6,0%	shopper profile, household size
Ice cream	Yes	vs. Tier 3: 28,4% vs. Tier 2: 24,8% vs. Brand: 11,9%	Yes	5,0%	shopper profile

<u>Research question 1 - The variance in WTP is at least partly explained by the perceived difference in packaging appeal, however differs by grocery category.</u>

The regression analysis for research question 1 (the relationship between difference in package scores and price premiums) showed a maximum adjusted R2 value of R2 = 0,345, indicating that 35% of variation are explained by the packaging. This score was achieved for the price premium between retailer brand Tier 1 and Tier 3 jams. Overall, the jam, ham and ice cream category had high % of explanation of the variation, with the only exception being ice cream Tier 1 versus branded and ham Tier 1 versus Tier 2. The cheese category overall scored lower indicating a lower level of variation explanation. Generally, the findings for research question 1 indicate that the difference in packaging appeal support a price premium, however it is not the sole driver as the maximum variance explanation of 35% indicates. Also a generalization across categories cannot be made, as the results for cheese are far below the other categories as well as the ice cream category is changing drastically if previous buyers are excluded.

Research question 2 – In none of the four categories there is a meaningful explanation of WTP of the Tier 1 product by the perceived packaging appeal

The regression outcomes for research question 2 (the relationship between packaging score and WTP for retailer brand Tier 1) were inconclusive. All four categories showed results that were technically statistically significant, but that had a very low predictive power. The highest adjusted R2 value observed in this category was $R^2 = 0{,}089$ (8.9%), for the cheese category. The overall finding of this test is that there is no meaningful difference in WTP based on the packaging attractiveness of the product as standalone driver.

Research question 3 – Demographics strongly impact WTP for the Tier 1 product, however are different across grocery categories. Most common the loyal shopper is willing to pay a significant higher price than the functional shopper.

For the third research question (demographic differences in WTP for Tier 1), the findings are very conclusive. Whilst gender was not a factor in any of the categories, the other demographics impacted the WTP statistically significant. For ham, older buyers had a higher WTP than younger buyers. Families had a lower WTP than single buyers. For cheese, lower income groups indicated a lower WTP than the 3,000 to 5,000 Euros per month income group. Loyal shoppers had a higher WTP than functional shoppers. For jam, families had a higher WTP than singles. Loyal buyers also had a higher WTP than functional shoppers in this category. Finally, for ice cream loyal buyers had a higher WTP than functional shoppers. Overall, it appears that the strongest consistent relationship between demographics and WTP is that loyal buyers have a higher WTP than functional buyers in most categories. Given this, the answer to the third research question is that there are differences between functional and loyal shoppers, with loyal shoppers being willing to pay more for products. However, other differences such as household size, age and household net income are less certain and more product-sensitive (e.g. Jam and Ham have different indications about household size WTP).

5. Conclusions and recommendations

5.1. Arrangement of the chapter

The following chapter identifies the main conclusions for each of the research questions which are derived from the review of the current literature as well as the quantitative analysis of the survey results. Succeeding, related recommendations for retailers will be presented. The chapter will conclude with recommendations for further areas of research.

5.2. Conclusions

The study was set out to explore the impact of product packaging on consumers' value perception, specifically if packaging enables retailers to take premium pricing with their retailer brand premium tier in the food segment in Germany. As shown in the literature retailer brands still have to overcome a consumer perceived barrier of risk which was partially overcome in the past via a low price versus the respective national brand. However, growth of the value retailer brands has stalled and retailers can only continue to grow market share by expanding their Tier 2 and Tier 1 premium offerings. As such, it is key for retailers to understand how they can justify the pricing premium of a Tier 1 product. For the aspect of packaging this has been explored leveraging the following sub-research questions:

1. Are consumers willing to pay a price premium for retailer brand Tier 1 products compared to branded and retailer brands Tier 2 / Tier 3 products based on the packaging appeal?

2. Do current retailer brand tier 1 premium priced products justify their price premium based on the packaging impression?

3. Are there demographic specifications such as gender, age, household size, household income or shopping behaviour influencing the willingness to pay a premium price?

The main empirical findings from the literature review (Chapter 2) and quantitative analysis of the survey (Chapter 4) were summarized within the respective chapter. The following will combine the findings of both with regards to the studys three research questions.

5.2.1. Conclusions for research question 1 – confirmed by literature review and analysis

The literature review confirmed that there is a strong relationship between pricing and packaging (*Brunso, K., et al. 2002*). Further, packaging is judged by consumers in-store depending on its shelf impact related to other products in the category and hence also serves as a consumer relevant mean of differentitation according to *Carpenter et al. (1994)*. Importantly, a key purchase barrier for retailer brands is the level of perceived risk *(Batra, R., Sinha, I. 2000)* which differs by product category.

This has been translated into the research question 1 and tested with a regression analysis based on the difference in packaging scores and difference in WTP (price premium) between the Tier 1 product and respective Tier 2/3 or branded product. The outcome shows for all categories but cheese a meaningful relationship which is statistically relevant, confirming the opinion in the literature (*Brunso, K., et al. 2002*). This indicates that packaging supports the price differentiation, however it is not the sole driver as the variance was only explained by up to 35%. Hence, there are other drivers such as brand equity or consumer loyalty underlying impacting the WTP. But importantly also the perceived risk is different by category and as such drives the difference in category results confirming *Batra, R., Sinha, I. (2000)*.

5.2.2. Conclusions for research question 2 – confirmed by literature review, but not analysis

Whilst the literature review confirms the close link of price and related sensory quality perception *(Deliza, R., MacFie, H. 1996)*, this has not been proven in the analysis of results of the research second question. The results of the regression analysis of packaging appeal and pricing of the retailer Tier 1 product did not provide a meaningful explanation of WTP for the Tier 1 product. As such a sole quality packaging will not support a substantial price premium as it is currently seen in-store. Interestingly, the mean price premium in the study is far below the actual price premium in-store, which confirms that the packaging alone seems not to be the sole driver for the price premium. Hence, only the combination of sensory quality aspects beyond packaging as indicated in the literature might have a meaningful relationship with the WTP.

5.2.3. Conclusions for research question 3 – confirmed by analysis

The analysis of the survey results confirmed that demographics have an impact on the WTP for the Tier 1 product. Therefore, segmentation of consumers will be essential to drive premium tier sales. Especially the loyal shopper is willing to spend statistically significantly more, which is confirmed for three of the four categories. Additionally, age (older buyers) as well as higher income are confirmed demographics to support a higher WTP. The household size will depend on the category as findings across categories have been opposite, i.e. once singles spending more (ham) and once families spending more (jam). This contradiction might be driven by the usage of the product i.e. given jam is sweet it might be eaten by the entire family and especially kids, whilst ham is rather favored by adults. Overall, targeting and segmentation is therefore a powerful tool for retailers to increase Tier 1 sales.

This research has shown that only parts of the premium pricing of retailer brand Tier 1 brands can be justified behind a higher packaging appeal. It remains key for retailers to continue to build also a brand equity for their premium retailer brands in order to continue to drive growth in that segment.

5.3. Recommendations for retailers

Retailers currently show a low level of trial in the retailer brand Tier 1 segment, as the survey revealed that across categories <10% of participants have previously purchased the premium product. This leads to the conclusion that the Tier 1 product is not yet targeted to a meaningful consumer segment. Based on the survey results retailers should drive a clear segmentation to enrich sales of Tier 1. The ideal prime prospect would be an older loyal shopper with a net income of >3000EUR, however gender and household size will not play a critical role. The key burden to overcome is to reach the loyal shopper who has an affinity for a proven brand and hence judgmentally perceives a higher risk in moving towards retailer brands as described by *Batra, R., Sinha, I. (2000)*. This will require the retailer to use his well established brand name to build trust with the consumer and provide him the assurance of offering a working product. Retailers might also drive risk mitigation leveraging the key advantage of owning the space in-store, by offering product sampling in-store. Alternatively, offering a smaller and therefore cheaper packaging size/ sample size might help to mitigate perceived risk.

Importantly, besides segmentation the packaging still needs to provide a premium quality impression to act as shelf decision maker, also based on the findings of *Silayoi, P., Speece, M. (2004)*.

5.4. Recommendations for further research

Future studies should focus on how retailers can attract the loyal brand loving shoppers as this will be the key burden to overcome. This is not an easy switching consumer, so tools like in-store sampling in order to establish a premium retailer brand Tier 1 equity need to be evaluated in terms of which have the highest success in driving trial and long term loyalty.

Additionally, age has been proven in one category to be a relevant driver for higher WTP. This could indicate the existence of a consumer life cycle across retailer brands as age and income develop (e.g. purchasing retailer brand Tier 3 in university, then up-tiering to retailer brand tier 2 and tier 1 as income increases over time). This requires a long term study starting with currently young participants and tracking them over time. Also the contradiction with regards to household size in the jam and ham category should be further investigated, if it is driven by the consumption of the product (kids or entire family for jam versus adults only for ham).

6. Bibliography

Abraham, S.; 2005; Stretching strategic thinking; Strategy and Leadership 33(5), pp.5-12

Ailawadi, K.L., Pauwels, K., Steenkamp, J.E.M; 2008; Private label use and store loyalty; Journal of Marketing, 72(6), pp.19-30

ARD; 2013; Der Edeka/Rewe-check; http://www.ardmediathek.de/das-erste/reportage-dokumentation /der-edeka-rewe-check?documentId=12976782 viewed on 05.05.2013

Ambrose, G., Harris, P.; 2011; Packaging the brand: Exploring the relationship between packaging design and brand identity; Lausanne, Switzerland: AVA Publishing

Ares, G., Besio, M., Gimenez, A., Deliza, R.; 2010; Relationship between involvement and functional milk desserts intention to purchase. Influence on attitude towards packaging characteristics; Appetite, 55, pp.298-304

Ares, G., Deliza, R.; 2010; Studying the influence of package shape and colour on consumer expectations of milk desserts using word association and conjoint analysis; Food Quality and Preference, 21, p.930-937

Batra, R., Sinha, I.; 2000; Consumer-level factors moderating the success of private label brands; Journal of Retailing, 76(2), pp.175-91

Bech-Larsen, T., Scholderer, J.; 2007; Functional foods in Europe: Consumer research, market experiences and regulatory aspects; Trends in Food Science and Technology, 18, pp.231-34

Becker, L., van Rompay, T.J.L., Schifferstein, H.N.J., Galetzka, M.; 2011; Tough package, strong taste: The influence of packaging design on taste impressions and product evaluations; Food Quality and Preference, 22, pp.17-23

Bellizzi, J.A., Hite, R.E.; 1992; Environmental color, consumer feelings and purchase likelihood; Psychology and Marketing, 9(5), pp.347-63

Berentzen, J.B.; 2010; Handelsmarkenmanagement: Solution selling in vertikalen Wertschöpfungsnetzwerken; Wiesbaden, Germany: Gabler

Blythe, J.; 2008; Essentials of marketing; Harlow, UK: Pearson Education

Bone, P.F., France, K.; 2001; Package graphics and consumer product beliefs; Journal of Business and Psychology, 15(3), pp.467-89

Brunso, K., Fjord, T.A., Grunert, K.G.; 2002; 77 Consumers' food choice and quality perception; Working Paper; Aarhus, Denmark: Aarhus School of Business

Carpenter, G.S., Glazer, R., Nakamoto K.; 1994; Meaningful brands from meaningless differentiation: the dependence on irrelevant attributes; Journal of Marketing Research 31, pp.339-350

Calver, G.; 2007; What is packaging design; Mies, Switzerland: Rotovision

Cheftel, J.C.; 2005; Food and nutrition labelling in the European Union; Food Chemistry, 93(3), pp.531-50

Chrsyochou, P., Askegaard, S., Grunert, K.G., Kristensen, D.B.; 2010; Social discourses of healthy eating. A market segmentation approach; Appetite, 55, pp.288-97

Costa, A.I.A., Jongen, W.M.F.; 2006; New insights into consumer-led food product development; Trends in Food Science and Technology, 17, pp.457-65

Dainelli, D. et al.; 2008; Active and intelligent food packaging: legal aspects and safety concerns; Trends in Food Safety and Technology, 19(1), pp.S103-12

Deliza, R., MacFie, H.; 1996; The generation of sensory expectation by external cues and its effect on sensory perception and hedonic ratings: A review; Journal of Sensory Studies, 11, pp.103-28

DelVecchio, D.; 2001; Consumer perceptions of private label quality: the role of product category characteristics and consumer use of heuristics; Journal of Retailing and Consumer Services, 8(5), pp.239-49

Drewniany, B.L., Jewler, A.J.; 2011; Creative Strategy in Advertising; Boston, MA: Wadsworth Cengage Learning

Floor, K.; 2006; Branding a store: How to build successful retail brands in a changing marketplace; London, UK: Kogan Page

Garrettson, J.A., Fisher, D., Burton, S.; 2002; Antecedents of private label attitude and national brand promotion attitude: similarities and differences; Journal of Retailing, 78, pp.91-99

GFK; 2012; Consumer index 12-2012; http://www.gfk.com/de/Documents/News%20Deutschland/GfK _Consumerindex_12_2012.pdf viewed online on 05.05.2013

Grimes, A., Doole, I.; 1998; Exploring the relationships between colour and international branding: A cross-cultural of the UK and Taiwan; Journal of Marketing Management, 14(7), pp.799-817

Grossman, R.P., Wisenblit, J.W.; 1999; What we know about consumers' color choices; Journal of Marketing Practice, 5(3), pp.78-88

Grunert, K.G., Baadsgaard, A., Larsen, H.H., Madsen, T.K.; 1996; Market Orientation in Food and Agriculture; Norwell, MA: Kluwer Academic Publishers

Gupta, S., Randhawa, G.; 2008; Retail management; New Dehli, India: Atlantic

Heckman, J.H.; 2005; Food packaging regulation in the United States and the European Union; Regulatory Toxicology and Pharmacology, 42, pp.96-122

Imram, N.; 1999; The role of visual cues in consumer perception and acceptance of a food product; Nutrition and Food Science, 5, pp.224-28

Klimchuk, M.R., Krasovec, S.A.; 2013; Packaging design: Successful branding from concept to shelf; Hoboken, NJ: John Wiley and Sons

Kumar, N., Steenkamp, J.B.; 2007; Private label strategy: How to meet the store brand challenge; Boston, USA: Harvard Business School Publishing

Lahteenmaki, L., Lampila, P., Grunert, K., Boztug, Y., Ueland, O., Aström, A., Martinsdottir, E.; 2010; Impact of health-related claims on the perception of other product attributes; Food Policy, 35, pp.230-39

Lamey, L., Deelersnyder, B., Dekimpe, M.G., Steenkamp, J.E.M.; 2007; How business cycles contribute to private-label success: Evidence from the United States and Europe; Journal of Marketing, 71(1), pp.1-15

Lebensmittelzeitung; 2013; Top 30 Lebensmittelhandel Deutschland 2013; http://www.lebensmittel zeitung.net/business/daten-fakten/rankings/Top-30-Lebensmittel-Handel-2013_371.html viewed online on 20.05.2013

Lincoln, K., Thomassen, L.; 2009; Private Label: Turning the Retail Brand Threat Into Your Biggest Opportunity; London, UK: Kogan Page

Marshall, D., Stuart, M., Bell, R.; 2006; Examining the relationship between product package colour and product selection in preschoolers; Food Quality and Preference, 17, pp.615-21

Marsh, K., Bugusu, B.; 2007; Food packaging - roles, materials and environmental issues; Journal of Food Science, 72(3), pp.R39-55

Mizutani, N. et al.; 2010; Package images modulate flavor perception for orange juice ; Food Quality and Preference, 21, pp.867-72

Murray, J.M., Delahunty, C.M.; 2000; Mapping consumer preference for the sensory and packaging attributes of Cheddar cheese; Food Quality and Preference, 11(5), pp.419-35

Nancarrow, G., Wright, L.T., Brace, I.; 1998; Gaining competitive advantage from packaging and labelling in marketing communications; British Food Journal, 100(2), pp.110-18

Pepe, M.S., Abratt, R., Dion, P.; 2012; Competitive advantage, private-label brands and category profitability; Journal of Marketing Management, 28(1-2), pp.154-72

Peters, J., Higgins, B., Richmond, M.; 2013; Creating value through packaging: Unlocking a new business and management strategy; Lancaster, USA: Destech Publications

Raghubir, P., Krishna, A.; 1999; Vital dimensions in volume perception: Can the eye fool the stomach?; Journal of Marketing Research, 36(3), pp.313-26

Rettie, R., Brewer, C.; 2000; The verbal and visual components of package design; Journal of Product and Brand Management, 9(1), pp.56-70

Richardson, P., Jain, A.K., Dick, A.; 1996; The influence of store aesthetics on evaluation of private label brands; Journal of Product and Brand Management, 5(1), pp.19-28

Rundh, B.; 2005; The multi-faceted dimension of packaging: Marketing logistic or marketing tool?; British Food Journal, 107(9), pp.670-84

Rundh, B.; 2009; Packaging design: Creating competitive advantage with product packaging; British Food Journal, 111(9), pp.988-1002

Saunders, M., Lewis, P., Thornhill, A.; 2009; Research methods for business students; London, UK: Pearson

Silayoi, P., Speece, M.; 2004; Packaging and purchase decisions: An exploratory study on the impact of involvement level and time pressure; British Food Journal, 106(8), pp.607-28

Sinha, I., Batra, R.; 1999; The effect of consumer price consciousness on private label purchase; International Journal of Research in Marketing, 16(3), pp.237-51

Statistisches Bundesamt; 2013; Entwicklung der Bruttoverdienste; https://www.destatis.de/DE/Zahlen Fakten/GesamtwirtschaftUmwelt/VerdiensteArbeitskosten/VerdiensteBranchen/Tabellen/LangeReiheD.ht ml?nn=50684 viewed online on 20.05.2013

Statistisches Bundesamt; 2013b; Haushalte nach Haushaltsgröße; https://www.destatis.de/DE/Zahlen Fakten/GesellschaftStaat/Bevoelkerung/HaushalteFamilien/Tabellen/Haushaltsgroesse.html viewed online on 20.05.2013

Steenkamp, J.E.M., Van Trijp, H.C.M.; 1996; Quality guidance: A consumer-based approach to quality improvement using partial least squares; European Review of Agricultural Economics, 23, pp.195-215

Sullivan, M., Adcock, D.; 2002; Retail marketing; London, UK: Thomson Learning

Underwood, R.L., Klein, N.M.; 2002; Packaging as brand communication: Effects of product pictures on consumer responses to the package and brand; Journal of Marketing Theory and Practice, 10(4), pp.58-68

Underwood, R.L., Ozanne, J.L.; 1998; Is your package an effective communicator? A normative framework for increasing the communicative competence of packaging; Journal of Marketing Communications, 4(4), pp.207-20

7. Appendix

7.1. Survey data results tables

Figure 37: Frequency table for gender distribution in the sample

Gender split	Frequency	%	Cumulative %
Female	72	45%	45%
Male	87	55%	100%
Total	159	100%	

Figure 38: Frequency table for age distribution in the sample

Age group	Frequency	%	Cumulative %
18 - 29	48	30%	30%
30 - 49	74	47%	77%
> 50	37	23%	100%
Total	159	100%	

Figure 39: Frequency table for net income distribution in the sample

Net Income	Frequency	%	Cumulative %
< 1000 Euro	27	17%	17%
1000 - 3000 Euro	79	50%	67%
3001 - 5000 Euro	23	14%	81%
> 5000 Euro	13	8%	89%
No answer	17	11%	100%
Total	159	100%	

Figure 40: Frequency table for household size distribution in the sample

Household size	Frequency	%	Cumulative %
1	54	34%	34%
2	65	41%	75%
3	23	14%	89%
4	13	8%	97%
5 and more	4	3%	100%
Total	159	100%	

Figure 41: Frequency table for self-descriptor of shopping behaviour in the sample

Shopper Type	Frequency	%	Cumulative %
Functional	74	47%	47%
Impulsive	37	23%	70%
Loyal	48	30%	100%
Total	159	100%	

Figure 42: Willingness to pay descriptive statistics for ham

Ham - Willigness to pay (€)				
		Retailer Brand		Branded
	Tier 3	Tier 2	Tier 1	Product
Mean	1,73	2,03	2,08	2,06
Std. Deviation	0,606	0,555	0,644	0,617

Figure 43: Price premium descriptive statistics for ham

Ham - Price Premium of Retailer Brand Tier 1 vs.			
	Retailer Brand		Branded
	Tier 3	Tier 2	Product
Mean	0,35	0,04	0,02
Std. Deviation	0,654	0,538	0,513

Figure 44: Packaging score descriptive statistics for ham

Ham - Packaging scores				
		Retailer Brand		Branded
	Tier 3	Tier 2	Tier 1	Product
Mean	2,92	3,95	3,57	4,03
Std. Deviation	1,326	1,237	1,399	1,387

Figure 45: Purchase frequency table for ham

Ham - Purchased in the past (% of total answers)				
		Retailer Brand		Branded
	Tier 3	Tier 2	Tier 1	Product
Yes	49,7%	17,6%	4,4%	34,0%
No	43,4%	78,6%	91,2%	61,6%
No answer	6,9%	3,8%	4,4%	4,4%

Figure 46: Summary of one-way ANOVA tests for willingness to pay for ham

Driver for differences in willingness to pay Tier 1 Retailer Brand		
Demograhic Category	F	Sig
Shopper profile	2,957	0,055
Gender	0,155	0,694
Age	3,956	0,021
Income	0,607	0,658
Household	4,114	0,018

Figure 47: Willingness to pay descriptive statistics for cheese

Cheese - Willigness to pay (€)				
		Retailer Brand		Branded
	Tier 3	Tier 2	Tier 1	Product
Mean	1,60	1,81	2,16	2,02
Std. Deviation	0,662	0,583	0,697	0,672

Figure 48: Price premium descriptive statistics for cheese

Cheese - Price Premium of Retailer Brand Tier 1 vs.		
	Retailer Brand		Branded
	Tier 3	Tier 2	Product
Mean	0,55	0,34	0,14
Std. Deviation	0,680	0,555	0,612

Figure 49: Packaging score descriptive statistics for cheese

Cheese - Packaging scores				
	Retailer Brand			Branded
	Tier 3	Tier 2	Tier 1	Product
Mean	3,02	3,39	3,67	3,57
Std. Deviation	1,329	1,185	1,349	1,371

Figure 50: Purchase frequency table for cheese

Cheese - Purchased in the past (% of total answers)				
	Retailer Brand			Branded
	Tier 3	Tier 2	Tier 1	Product
Yes	32,7%	16,4%	3,1%	35,2%
No	64,2%	79,2%	92,5%	57,2%
No answer	3,1%	4,4%	4,4%	7,5%

Figure 51: Summary of one-way ANOVA tests for willingness to pay for cheese

Driver for differences in willingness to pay Tier 1 Retailer Brand		
Demograhic Category	F	Sig
Shopper profile	3,079	0,049
Gender	2,81	0,096
Age	2,297	0,104
Income	3,337	0,012
Household	2,191	0,115

Figure 52: Willingness to pay descriptive statistics for jam

Jam - Willigness to pay (€)				
	Retailer Brand			Branded
	Tier 3	Tier 2	Tier 1	Product
Mean	1,65	1,99	1,98	2,10
Std. Deviation	0,622	0,615	0,639	0,624

Figure 53: Price premium descriptive statistics for jam

Jam - Price Premium of Retailer Brand Tier 1 vs.		
	Retailer Brand		Branded
	Tier 3	Tier 2	Product
Mean	0,32	-0,01	-0,12
Std. Deviation	0,570	0,498	0,539

Figure 54: Packaging score descriptive statistics for jam

Jam - Packaging scores				
		Retailer Brand		Branded
	Tier 3	Tier 2	Tier 1	Product
Mean	3,16	3,91	3,78	4,24
Std. Deviation	1,266	1,166	1,251	1,219

Figure 55: Purchase frequency table for jam

Jam - Purchased in the past (% of total answers)				
		Retailer Brand		Branded
	Tier 3	Tier 2	Tier 1	Product
Yes	30,2%	15,1%	8,2%	57,2%
No	61,6%	78,6%	84,9%	37,7%
No answer	8,2%	6,3%	6,9%	5,0%

Figure 56: Summary of one-way ANOVA tests for willingness to pay for jam

Driver for differences in willingness to pay Tier 1 Retailer Brand		
Demograhic Category	F	Sig
Shopper profile	3,919	0,022
Gender	1,236	0,268
Age	2,537	0,082
Income	2,331	0,058
Household	3,113	0,047

Figure 57: Willingness to pay descriptive statistics for ice cream

Ice cream - Willigness to pay (€)				
		Retailer Brand		Branded
	Tier 3	Tier 2	Tier 1	Product
Mean	1,89	2,29	2,30	2,62
Std. Deviation	0,714	0,631	0,700	0,717

Figure 58: Price premium descriptive statistics for ice cream

Ice cream - Price Premium of Retailer Brand Tier 1 vs.			
		Retailer Brand	Branded
	Tier 3	Tier 2	Product
Mean	0,41	0,01	-0,32
Std. Deviation	0,715	0,570	0,513

Figure 59: Packaging score descriptive statistics for ice cream

Ice cream - Packaging scores				
		Retailer Brand		Branded
	Tier 3	Tier 2	Tier 1	Product
Mean	2,9	3,84	4,09	4,43
Std. Deviation	1,274	1,163	1,118	1,199

Figure 60: Purchase frequency table for ice cream

Ice cream - Purchased in the past (% of total answers)			
	Retailer Brand		Branded
	Tier 3	Tier 2	Tier 1	Product
Yes	29,6%	23,9%	6,9%	42,8%
No	64,2%	66,7%	87,4%	50,3%
No answer	6,3%	9,4%	5,7%	6,9%

Figure 61: Summary of one-way ANOVA tests for willingness to pay for ice cream

Driver for differences in willingness to pay Tier 1 Retailer Brand		
Demograhic Category	F	Sig
Shopper profile	3,863	0,023
Gender	0,081	0,776
Age	0,953	0,388
Income	2,017	0,095
Household	0,855	0,427

Figure 62: Comparison of research question 1 results between all participants and no previous purchase participants

	Question 1 (all participants) Packaging and price premium regression		Question 1 (only participants with no purchase) Packaging and price premium regression		
	Significant	Variation explained	Significant	Variation explained	Difference
Ham	Yes	vs. Tier 3: 19,4% vs. Tier 2: 12,7% vs. Brand: 20,3%	Yes	vs. Tier 3: 13,7% vs. Tier 2: 19,0% vs. Brand: 22,8%	vs. Tier 3: -5,7% vs. Tier 2: +6,3% vs. Brand: +2,5%
Cheese	Yes	vs. Tier 3: 15,1% vs. Tier 2: 5,6% vs. Brand: 15,0%	Yes	vs. Tier 3: 12,5% vs. Tier 2: 11,6% vs. Brand: 14,3%	vs. Tier 3: -2,6% vs. Tier 2: +6,0% vs. Brand: -0,7%
Jam	Yes	vs. Tier 3: 34,5% vs. Tier 2: 20,2% vs. Brand: 21,0%	Yes	vs. Tier 3: 30,3% vs. Tier 2: 17,9% vs. Brand: 5,2%	vs. Tier 3: -4,2% vs. Tier 2: -2,3% vs. Brand: -15,8%
Ice cream	Yes	vs. Tier 3: 28,4% vs. Tier 2: 24,8% vs. Brand: 11,9%	Yes	vs. Tier 3: 12,5% vs. Tier 2: 17,8% vs. Brand: 8,3%	vs. Tier 3: -15,9% vs. Tier 2: -7,0% vs. Brand: -3,6%

7.2. Online survey translation to English

Dear Participant:

Thank you for participating in this survey as part of my master thesis. Your personal information will not be collected for this survey and all results will be evaluated anonymous.

Once again, thank you for agreeing to participate in this survey. If you are ready to consent to participate, please click "Continue" below to begin the survey.

Question 1 (must be answered with myself to continue):

Who generally decides about the grocery purchases for your household?

Multiple choice:

- **Myself**
- **My partner**
- **Other**

Question 2 (must be answered Germany):

Where do you live:

Multiple choice:

- **Germany**
- **Other country**

Question 3:

Please read the following statements carefully and mark the one which generally describes your grocery purchase behaviour best:

Multiple choice:

- **I consider myself to be a very spontaneous shopper and often buy products that I didn't plan to. I choose the product that has good reputation, even if I pay more**
- **As long as the product works, I care less about the brand, more about the price**
- **I normally go for products that are proven to work well and brands I trust.**

Question 4 - 19:

Please carefully review the above shown products and please answer the following three questions for each product:

- **Picture 1: ja! Delikatess Kochschinken**
- **Picture 2: REWE Delikatess Metzgerschinken**
- **Picture 3: Herta Finesse**
- **Picture 4: REWE Feine Welt Würzig-zarter Schinkenbraten aus der Toskana**

Assuming the product meets your requirements, how much would you be willing to pay for it?

Slider:

0,50€ - 5,00€

How appealing do you find the respective product?

Multiple choice scale:

1 (not appealing) - 6 (strongly appealing)

Have you purchased this product in the past already?

Multiple choice:

- **Yes**
- **No**
- **Prefer not to answer**

(If previous answer is Yes) Has the product met your taste expectation?

Multiple choice:

- **Yes**
- **No**
- **Prefer not to answer**

Question 20 - 35:

Please carefully review the above shown products and please answer the following three questions for each product:

- **Picture 1: Schwartau Extra-Erdbeere**
- **Picture 2: ja! Erdbeere Konfitüre Extra**
- **Picture 3: REWE Feine Welt Sonnige Erdbeere**
- **Picture 4: REWE Konfitüre Extra Erdbeere**

Assuming the product meets your requirements, how much would you be willing to pay for it?

Slider:

0,50€ - 5,00€

How appealing do you find the respective product?

Multiple choice scale:

1 (not appealing) - 6 (strongly appealing)

Have you purchased this product in the past already?

Multiple choice:

- **Yes**
- **No**
- **Prefer not to answer**

(If previous answer is Yes) Has the product met your taste expectation?

Multiple choice:

- **Yes**
- **No**
- **Prefer not to answer**

Question 36 - 51:

Please carefully review the above shown products and please answer the following three questions for each product:

- **Picture 1: REWE Feine Welt Elsässer Genuss franz. Weichkäse mit fleur de biere**
- **Picture 2: Champignon Camembert**
- **Picture 3: REWE Weichkäse**
- **Picture 4: ja! Camembert**

Assuming the product meets your requirements, how much would you be willing to pay for it?

Slider:

0,50€ - 5,00€

How appealing do you find the respective product?

Multiple choice scale:

1 (not appealing) - 6 (strongly appealing)

Have you purchased this product in the past already?

Multiple choice:

- **Yes**
- **No**
- **Prefer not to answer**

(If previous answer is Yes) Has the product met your taste expectation?

Multiple choice:

- **Yes**
- **No**
- **Prefer not to answer**

Question 52 - 67:

Please carefully review the above shown products and please answer the following three questions for each product:

- **Picture 1: REWE Eis Bourbon Vanille**
- **Picture 2: REWE Feine Welt Pures Vergnügen Bourbon Vanille**
- **Picture 3: ja! Bourbon Vanille-Eis**
- **Picture 4: Mövenpick Bourbon Vanille**

Assuming the product meets your requirements, how much would you be willing to pay for it?

Slider:

0,50€ - 5,00€

How appealing do you find the respective product?

Multiple choice scale:

1 (not appealing) - 6 (strongly appealing)

Have you purchased this product in the past already?

Multiple choice:

- **Yes**
- **No**
- **Prefer not to answer**

(If previous answer is Yes) Has the product met your taste expectation?

Multiple choice:

- **Yes**
- **No**
- **Prefer not to answer**

Please provide a few statistical facts about yourself. Those will be exclusively used for a statistical analysis and don't allow any conclusion on an individual person.

Question 68:

You are:

Multiple choice:

- **Female**
- **Male**

Question 69:

Please specify your age group?

Multiple choice:

- **18-29**
- **30-49**
- **50 or older**

Question 70:

How many person are part of your household (including yourself)?

Multiple choice:

- **1**
- **2**
- **3**
- **4**
- **5 or more**

Question 71:

Your monthly net income (of all household members) is in the range of:

Multiple choice:

- **below 1000€**
- **1000€-1500€**
- **1500€-2000€**
- **2000€-2500€**
- **above 2500€**

Printed in Great Britain
by Amazon